BOATHOUSES OF BRITAIN

MICHAEL DAWSON

AMBERLEY

About the Author

Michael Dawson is an archaeologist, former heritage consultant and lecturer. He has lectured for the Department of Continuing Education, Oxford University, is a former Heritage Director at RPS and presently editor of the journal *Historic Environment Policy and Practice.*

First published 2025

Amberley Publishing
The Hill, Stroud,
Gloucestershire, GL5 4EP

www.amberley-books.com

ISBN: 978 1 3981 2181 2 (print)
ISBN: 978 1 3981 2182 9 (ebook)

British Library Cataloguing in Publication Data.
A catalogue record for this book is available from the British Library.

Typeset in 10pt on 13pt Celeste.
Origination by Amberley Publishing.
Printed in the UK.

Appointed GPSR EU Representative: Easy Access System Europe Oü, 16879218
Address: Mustamäe tee 50, 10621, Tallinn, Estonia
Contact Details: gpsr.requests@easproject.com, +358 40 500 3575

Contents

Acknowledgements

I would like to thank all those who have so generously contributed during the gestation of this book, especially Philip Brindle, John and Fiona Fells, Richard and Susan Jebb, Andy MacEwan, Joe Prentice, Tim and Claire Mitchell, Zoe Traill, and my late wife Judith for their insights, advice and suggestions. Any errors in the narrative are my responsibility.

Most photographs in this book were taken by the author between 2014 and 2024. The pre-war postcard of Hastings and the lithograph of the Oxford University Boat Club are from the author's collection. The painted illustrations are by the architect, author and artist Ian Robert Davis, and the map is by Andy Isham. All other image sources are acknowledged in the captions and are reproduced with thanks.

Introduction

On 4 August 1883 Everleigh Down, a twenty-one-year-old lieutenant in the Surrey militia, wanted to go fishing. After breakfast he and his brother Reginald went to the carpenter's shop, which was a dusty room at the Normansfield Hospital near Richmond-upon-Thames. Their father, Dr John Langdon Down, had set up the hospital on the north bank of the Thames at Hampton Wick to treat children with a condition that later became known as Down's syndrome. Reginald (seventeen) began turning a piece of brass, but Everleigh, a keen angler, was impatient to get out on the river. He snatched the brass, threw it to the floor and hit it repeatedly with a hammer. Reginald, angry with his brother, kicked him in the shin.

No one knows exactly what happened next, but according to the *Surrey Comet* Everleigh fell to the floor 'bleeding so severely that blood gushed through his clothes on to the shavings on the floor'. The doctor came within half an hour. He tied all the blood vessels and closed the wound. When Everleigh came round from the chloroform, he had no pulse. He died the following day. Dr Down raced home from Paris to attend an inquest for his dead son in his hospital dining room. Presented with the evidence, the jury deliberated for ten minutes before returning a verdict of accidental death.

The next year the Normansfield boathouse opened and, although not explicit in any record I could find, it was almost certainly a memorial to Everleigh Down. In his biography of Langdon Down, Dr Conor Ward described how 'both he and his sons had an enduring interest in the river and the Normansfield boathouse remains as a memorial to this special feature of the life of the Langdon Down family'.

In 2014, I was asked to assess the boathouse for a commercial developer. I found an ornate late Victorian building with a tiled roof, stained-glass windows and balcony overlooking the river. There was a panelled room and small kitchen above a boat bay. The proposal was to move the boathouse back from the river 50 metres and replace it with a five-storey yacht-inspired home, a sort of Sydney Opera House on the Thames. Apparently, Renzo Piano, the avant-garde Italian architect, liked the concept.

Research showed the Velma boathouse was the former Normansfield Hospital boathouse. Children were cared for in a family setting rather than a grim Victorian asylum. It was a rare survival, in almost original condition, associated with a significant historic event and an important individual. Its heritage significance was quickly appreciated, and it was listed Grade II*.

The Velma boathouse may be just another story of an unsuccessful development proposal. On the other hand, the complex paper trail that identified the architect, the owner and the role played by the building in the treatment of damaged children, and the tragic death the boathouse commemorated, highlighted the lack of research into this class of building.

The more you look, the more you find. Buildings are not passive. We walk among them, make homes of them, use them for work and play, talk about and value them. Surprisingly, almost nothing has been published about boathouses. An architectural summary by the architect Clare Sherrif describes boathouses along the Thames between Oxford and Richmond; Adam Menuge in 2010 described the Lakeland boathouses during the early nineteenth century, based on his work for the National Trust; and Colin and Paula Martin looked at boathouses on the Sound of Mull.

Boathouses are occasionally of marginal interest, but nobody knows how many boathouses there are. The National Heritage list includes over 102 designated boathouses, but in the late 1900s there were over 300 lifeboat stations each with their own, often architect-designed, lifeboat house. There are coastguard stations; naval boathouses, where ships' boats were made and maintained; rowing clubs; parks; and great estates. There are ecclesiastical palaces with boathouses, even duck decoys with boathouses, before we reach those on canals, broads, meres, flashes and estuaries that characterise our towns and countryside. In the days of sail, wooden boats and ships, boathouses were critical. Hauling a boat ashore for the winter helped control the wood-boring sea snail. Pitching, caulking and repair kept ships and boats at sea during the summer. Boathouses were not just there for boats. They stored equipment, materials, tools and weapons. Dante, in *Inferno*, likened them to the dark boiling fires of Hell.

This book offers a brief introduction to a building type too long neglected. Boathouses form part of our valued landscapes. They are reminders of aristocratic fashion and key factors in saving lives at sea. Sporting boathouses have also evolved, from a publican's outhouse to a clubhouse to an Olympic venue. In our modern world a boathouse is about recreation, entertainment, holidays, social aspiration and sometimes a place of work. Look beyond the surface and boathouses represent social change, economic success, community value, inclusivity and sustainability. This short book is the first of its kind. It starts with the Roman invasion and ends with Olympic gold. I hope it inspires a re-evaluation of the boathouse in our everyday life, highlighting its variety and sometimes innovative design, providing a snapshot of its value in art and literature, drama and competition. Here is an opportunity to see a familiar building in a new light, which, until now, has been hidden in plain sight.

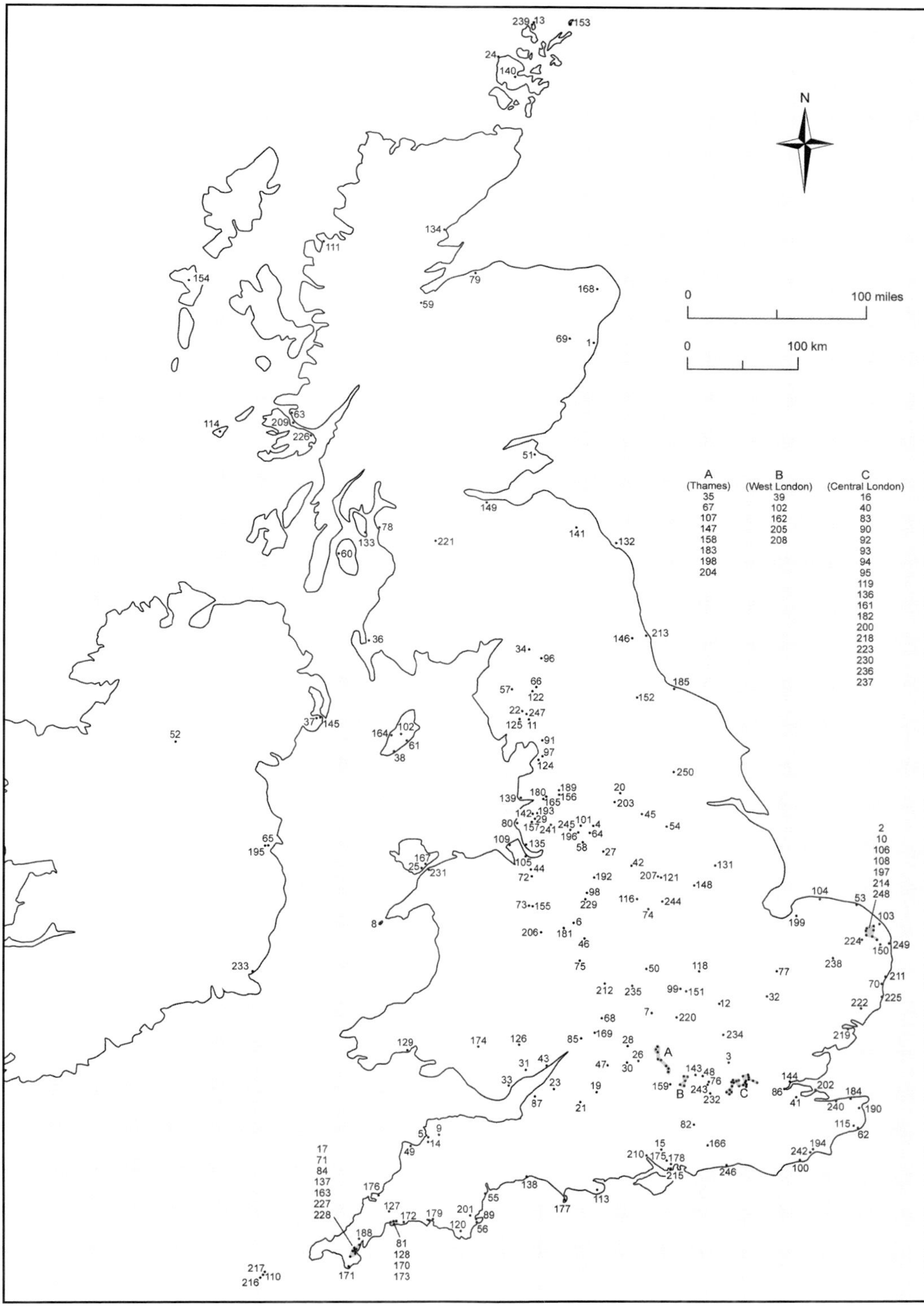

Locations of places mentioned in the text.

1. Aberdeen
2. Acle, Norfolk
3. Aldenham, Hertfordshire
4. Alexandra Park, Oldham, Lancashire
5. Appledore, Devon
6. Aqualate Mere, Staffordshire
7. Banbury, Oxfordshire
8. Bardsey Island, Gwynedd
9. Barnstaple, Devon
10. Barton Broad, Norfolk
11. Belle Isle, Windermere, Cumbria
12. Bedford, Bedfordshire
13. Binnaskirk, Papa Westray, Orkney
14. Bideford, Devon
15. Bishops Waltham, Hampshire
16. Blackfriars, London
17. Bosahan, Helford River, Cornwall
18. Boulogne, France – not Illustrated
19. Bowood Wiltshire
20. Bradford, Yorkshire
21. Bradford-on-Avon, Wiltshire
22. Brathay, Windemere, Cumbria
23. Bristol, Avon
24. Brough of Birsay, Orkney
25. Brynsiencyn, Menai Straits, Anglesey
26. Buckland House, Oxfordshire
27. Bugworth, Derbyshire
28. Burford, Oxfordshire
29. Burscough, Lancashire
30. Buscot Park, Oxfordshire
31. Caerleon, Gwent
32. Cambridge, Cambridgeshire
33. Cardiff, Gwent
34. Carlisle, Cumbria
35. Carmel College, Wallingford, Oxfordshire
36. Castle Kennedy, Loch Insh, Dumfries and Galloway
37. Castle Ward, Downpatrick
38. Castletown, Isle of Man
39. Caversham, Berkshire
40. Charing Cross, London
41. Chatham, Kent
42. Chatsworth, Derbyshire
43. Chepstow, Monmouthshire
44. Chester, Cheshire
45. Chevet Hall, Wakefield, West Yorkshire
46. Chillington Park, Staffordshire
47. Cleveland Lakes, Wiltshire
48. Cliveden, Cookham, Buckinghamshire
49. Clovelly, Devon
50. Combe Abbey, Coventry, Warwickshire
51. Craigttoun Park, St Andrews, Fife
52. Crom Castle, Co. Fermanagh
53. Cromer, Norfolk
54. Cusworth, Doncaster, South Yorkshire
55. Dawlish, Devon
56. Dartmouth, Devon
57. Derwent Isle, Cumbria
58. Didsbury, Greater Manchester
59. Dochfour House, Inverness
60. Dougarie, Isle of Arran
61. Douglas, Isle of Man
62. Dover, Kent
63. Drimin, Sound of Mull
64. Droyslden, Greater Manchester
65. Dublin, Leinster
66. Duke of Portland's Boathouse, Ullswater, Cumbria
67. Cherwell Boathouse, Oxford
68. Dumbleton, Gloucestershire
69. Dunecht, Aberdeenshire
70. Dunwich, Suffolk
71. Durghan, Helford River, Cornwall
72. Eaton Hall Park, Cheshire
73. Ellesmere, Shropshire
74. Elvaston, Derbyshire
75. Enville, Shropshire
76. Eton, Berkshire
77. Ely, Cambridgeshire
78. Fairlie, Firth of Clyde, North Ayrshire
79. Findhorn, Moray Firth, Moray
80. Formby, Lancashire
81. Fowey, Cornwall
82. Frensham Great Pond, Surrey
83. Furnivall, Lower Mall, London
84. Glendurgan, Helford River, Cornwall
85. Gloucester, Gloucestershire
86. Gravesend, Kent
87. Great Wemberham, Yatton, Somerset

88. Greenwich, London
89. Greenway, Devon
90. Gunnersbury Park, London
91. Hale, Lancashire
92. Hampton, London
93. Hampton Wick, London
94. Hampton Court, London
95. Hammersmith, London
96. Hallsteads, Cumbria
97. Halton on Lune, Lancashire
98. Hanley Park, Stoke-on-Trent, Staffordshire
99. Harlestone Park, Northamptonshire
100. Hastings, Kent
101. Heaton Park, Greater Manchester
102. Henley, Oxfordshire
103. Hickling, Norfolk
104. Holkham, Norfolk
105. Hooton Park, Cheshire
106. Hoveton, Norfolk
107. Howbury Park, Crowmarsh Gifford, Oxfordshire
108. How Hill, Norfolk
109. HoylakeWirral
110. Hugh Town, Isles of Scilly
111. Isle of Ewe
112. Isle of Man
113. Isle of Purbeck
114. Isle of Tiree (Scarinish)
115. Kearsey Court (Russell Park), Dover, Kent
116. Kedleston, Derbyshire
117. Kelmscott, Oxfordshire
118. Kettering, Northamptonshire
119. Kew Wharf, London
120. Kingsbridge, Devon
121. Kingsmill, Nottinghamshire
122. Lake District, Cumbria
123. Lambeth, London
124. Lancaster, Lancashire
125. Lanehead, Coniston Water, Cumbria
126. Lanfoist, Monmouthshire
127. Lanhydrock, Cornwall
128. Lanteglos-by-Fowey, Cornwall
129. Laugharne, Carmarthenshire
130. Limehouse, River Thames, Essex
131. Lincoln, Lincolnshire
132. Lindisfarne Abbey, Northumberland
133. Little Cumbrae Isle, North Ayrshire
134. Littleferry, Sutherland
135. Liverpool Princes Park, Sefton Park, Merseyside
136. London (see map list C)
137. Lower Greatwood, Carrick Roads, Falmouth
138. Lyme Regis, Dorset
139. Lytham St Annes, Lancashire
140. Mainland, Orkney
141. Manderston, Berwick
142. Martin Mere, Lancashire
143. Marlow Thames
144. Mucking, Thames Estuary, London
145. Myra Castle, Strangford Loch
146. Newcastle upon Tyne, Tyne and Wear
147. Nuneham Courtney, Oxfordshire
148. Newark-on-Trent, Nottinghamshire
149. Newton Point, Scottish Highlands
150. Norfolk Broads, Norfolk
151. Northampton, Northamptonshire
152. North Lodge, Darlington, Co. Durham
153. North Ronaldsay
154. North Uist
155. Oteley, Shropshire
156. Osbaldeston, Lancashire
157. Ormskirk, Lancashire
158. Oxford, Oxfordshire
159. Pangbourne, Berkshire
160. Papa Westray, Orkney
161. Paris Garden, London
162. Park Place, near Henley, Berkshire
163. Pedn Billy, Helford River, Cornwall
164. Peel, Isle of Man
165. Penwortham, Lancashire
166. Petworth, West Sussex
167. Plas Newydd, Anglesey
168. Pitfour, Scotland, Aberdeenshire
169. Pittville, Cheltenham, Gloucestershire
170. Polkerris, Cornwall
171. Polpeor Cove, Cornwall
172. Polperro, Cornwall

173. Polruan, Cornwall
174. Porth yr Ogof, Powys
175. Porchester, Hampshire
176. Port Isaac, Cornwall
177. Portland, Dorset
178. Portsmouth, Hampshire
179. Plymouth, Devon
180. Preston and River Ribble, Lancashire
181. Preston upon the Weald Moors, Shropshire
182. Putney, London
183. Radley, Oxfordshire
184. Reculver, Kent
185. Redcar, North Yorkshire
186. Redhouse Public House, Battersea, London
187. Regents Park, London
188. Restronguet Point, Cornwall
189. Ribchester, Lancashire
190. Richborough, Kent
191. Richmond upon Thames, London
192. Rudyard Lake, Staffordshire
193. Rufford, Lancashire
194. Rye, East Sussex
195. Safehaven, Dublin, Co. Cork
196. Salford, Greater Manchester
197. Salhouse, Norfolk
198. Salters, Oxford
199. Sandringham, Norfolk
200. Scotland Yard, London
201. Sharpham, Devon
202. Sheerness, Kent
203. Shibden, Halifax, West Yorkshire
204. Shillingford, Oxfordshire
205. Shiplake, Henley, Oxfordshire
206. Shrewsbury, Shropshire
207. Skegby, Lincolnshire
208. Sonning, River Thames, Berkshire
209. Sound of Mull
210. Southampton, Hampshire
211. Southwold, Suffolk
212. South Crest, Redditch, Worcestershire
213. South Shields, Tyne and Wear
214. South Walsham, Norfolk
215. Spithead, Portsmouth, Hampshire
216. St Agnes, Isles of Scilly
217. St Mary's, Isles of Scilly
218. Stangate, London
219. Stour (River), Suffolk
220. Stowe, Buckingham
221. Stratsteven, Avondale
222. Sutton Hoo, Suffolk
223. Teddington, London
224. Thorpe St Andrew, Suffolk
225. Thorpeness, Suffolk
226. Torosay, Sound of Mull
227. Trebah, Helford River, Cornwall
228. Trelawarren, Cornwall
229. Trentham Gardens, Staffordshire
230. Vauxhall Cross, Greater London
231. Vaynol Estate, Gwynedd
232. Virginia Water, Greater London
233. Wexford, County Wexford
234. Wardown Park, Luton, Bedfordshire
235. Warwick Castle, Warwickshire
236. Westminster, London
237. Whitehall, London
238. Whitelodge, Norfolk
239. Whitehowe, Papa Westray, Orkney
240. Whitstable, Kent
241. Wigan, Lancashire
242. Winchelsea, East Sussex
243. Windsor, Berkshire
244. Wollaton Park, Nottinghamshire
245. Worsley, Lancashire
246. Worthing, West Sussex
247. Wray Castle, Lake District, Cumbria
248. Wroxham, Norfolk
249. Great Yarmouth, Norfolk
250. York, Yorkshire

1

Invasion and Response

When the Romans invaded Britain in AD 43, they sailed from Boulogne. It was a huge undertaking; between 800 and 900 ships carried an army of 40,000 legionaries, cavalry horses, baggage animals, heavy equipment and rations. It took two years to assemble the invasion fleet in northern France. Boathouses, called 'shipsheds' in the Mediterranean, were essential for construction and maintenance. They may have been built at the port of Boulogne and on the banks of nearby rivers and inlets. The invaders secured a beachhead, probably at Richborough. Although no boathouses have been found there, temporary

Trajan's Column, a memorial to the emperor Trajan's war against the Dacians (modern Romania) in the second century AD. Scene LXXIX shows vaulted boatsheds above the head of the emperor Trajan (in the centre of the image). Boathouses were essential to keep the Roman fleet at sea. (www.trajanscolumn.org)

structures may have been built or the galleys returned to Boulogne to refit. In the winter, the warships were brought ashore and, under cover, cleaned, caulked, and pitched. Slipping, when a ship is drawn up on a slipway, and drying in a boathouse, *navalia,* were essential to reduce the impact of *Teredo navalis,* the maritime woodworm.

Roman Britain

Roman boathouses are dynamic buildings. They housed the largest mobile structures in the empire. Good design was critical to avoid damage due to the length and structure of the ships when moving from water to dry land. In the boathouse, the slipway would have been inclined and the roofline would have risen in parallel to the slipway or in steps. A gradient is essential because of the difficulty of launching a heavy ship; approximately 5° was sufficient to bring the ships ashore safely, to avoid sticking if too shallow or tipping if the buoyancy and gradient were not matched.

Launching a ship from the inclined slipway of a boathouse at the wrong time could result in major structural damage. The hull is not designed to support the weight of the ship out of water. If the ships tips at the point of transition, there is a potentially catastrophic strain placed on its straight keel.

Boathouses had to be well ventilated so hulls could dry out to prevent fungal rot. Light and air could have been let in by louvred tiled roofs, stepped roofs or sloping roofs, while colonnades or pillars improved access, lighting and ventilation. The scale of the boathouses depended on the ships they housed. For large Roman triremes, the sheds were over 7 × 40 metres long and up to 6.5 metres high. Inside the ship's keel slid along a greased wooden rail, fixed along the central groundway, which helped movement within the boathouse itself.

This mosaic, discovered in the garden of Palazzo Rospigliosi Pallavicini, Rome, in 1876, shows a Roman ship leaving port. The lighthouse and the arcades of the boatsheds identify the port as Alexandria, Egypt. (Centrale Montemartini Museum, Rome)

The difficulties in moving a galley of 40 tonnes, even a smaller liburnian at perhaps 7 tonnes, cannot be underestimated; consequently, building the boathouse in the correct location was critical. When slipping, the stern would need to be lined up with the boathouse and slipway. The vessel would have to be kept upright as it was hauled ashore. Launching a long ship required 'walking shores' as it was hauled down to the sea, a skilled operation even on a greased wooden slipway.

In the north, where there is a significant tidal range, boathouse design was an important factor for the Romans who were used to the Mediterranean. The boathouses would have been sited above the high watermark on riverbank or shoreline to avoid flooding. If the ship began to float it was in danger of damaging the sides or even the roof of the building. This could be avoided by ballasting, weighting the bows to hold them in place, but launching would probably have been impossible when a river or tide was in flood.

Bringing boats ashore or launching ships from land is almost impossible across a running stream. As a ship moves out of a boathouse it becomes increasingly difficult to control. Once the hull is afloat there is serious danger of it being swept away. Bringing boats ashore would have been even more difficult, since on a flowing stream it would have been quite impossible to line up the stern on the groundway. Consequently, boathouses were located so that ships were launched downstream or into a basin cut into the banks.

Typically, boathouses probably housed the oars – up to 170 for a trireme – and other necessary equipment. It was important to keep the oars clean and free of debris, to check for signs of bending or warping and properly lubricate moving surfaces to prevent wear. When stored, the oars needed to be dry and cool to prevent warping. They could be stored horizontally or vertically, but off the ground with the blades elevated. They may have been waxed when used in salty water.

Military boathouses would have been built for the Classis Britannia, the fleet formed after the invasion and stationed at Dover (Portus Dubris) and Boulogne (Gesericorum/Bononia). The remains of the earliest boathouses in Britain almost certainly lie below modern Dover, situated outside the naval fortress.

Looking seaward on the River Dour estuary from Roman Dover. This artist's impression of boatsheds reflects designs common in the Mediterranean. They were probably built where the fleet Classis Britannica was stationed in the first and second centuries AD. The boatsheds may have been similar to those at Portus (port of Rome) in Italy. (Ian Robert Davis)

Roman rule was secured by strategically placed forts and fortresses, many commanding an important river. At Caerleon, on the River Usk, founded in AD 74, boathouses were probably built close to the quayside, parallel to the river. They would have housed military patrol boats or supply vessels called *Naves onerariae*. At Carlisle, on the River Eden, a dedication to Mars, the god of war, by a unit of lightermen hints at the need for boathouses to maintain and protect these flat-bottomed boats.

Sailing boats were the workhorses of the northern seaways, but like the warships they had to be maintained. At Mucking, on the Thames estuary, a boathouse was excavated in 2009. It was an elongated U shape formed of twelve oak piles, open to the south-east, facing a silted estuarine channel. Erosion had removed any floor surface, but the main posts were 2 metres apart clad by weatherboarding. It was approximately 13 × 7 metres – enough for a small cargo boat.

On the Bristol Channel another coastal boathouse is an integral part of a villa at Great Wemberham in Somerset. Built of stone and possibly tiled, it is on a silted meander of the River Yeo. Excavation suggests the boat bay was dry and dates to the later third or early fourth century. Like Mucking, it was large enough to shelter a small sailing boat.

In the third century, raiding from the North Sea changed the nature of coastal defence. A series of Roman forts in the south and east, known as the Saxon Shore, formed a military district defending major rivers. Fixed defence in depth, with good communication links and mobile forces ready to attack, the forts were supported by a fleet able to move troops

Reconstruction of an early Roman boathouse at Stanford Wharf Nature Reserve, near Mucking, Essex, on the lower Thames. The boathouse probably housed the equipment and sails of a small cargo vessel. (Ian Robert Davis)

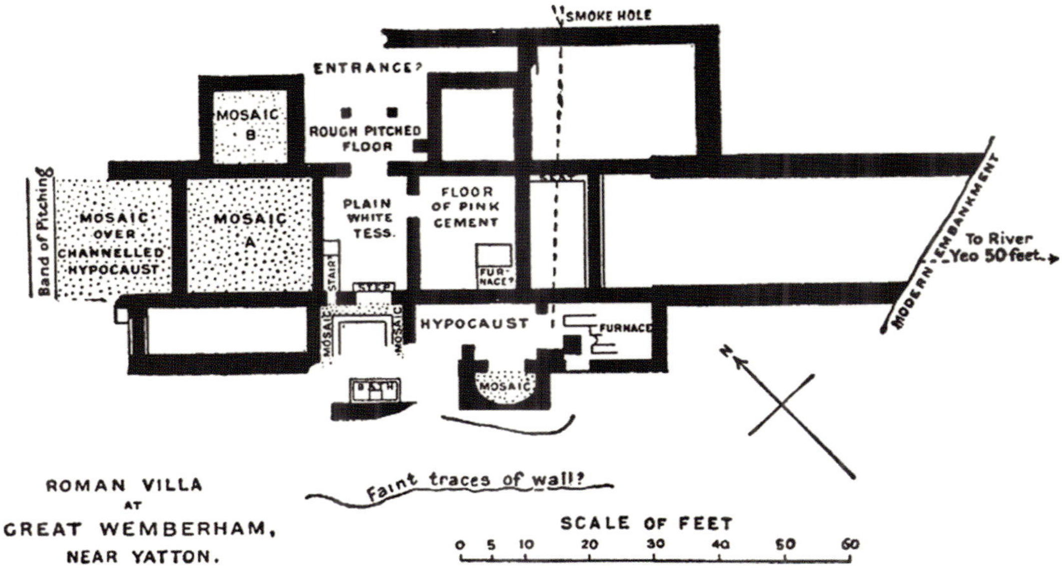

Plan of the Roman villa and boathouse at Great Wemberham. The villa has an entrance on the north side with an outer and an inner hall, a bathhouse and a staircase to lofts or upper story. The boathouse is an integral part of the villa on the north bank of the River Yeo.

Reconstruction of the boathouse at Great Wemberham, Somerset. The boathouse may have been similar to much later designs. It probably housed a pleasure boat or fishing skiff. (Ian Robert Davis)

quickly and confront the raiders. The remains of boathouses probably lie beneath the meres, mud flats or modern urban hinterlands of forts such as Porchester, Burgh Castle or Reculver. Boathouses to maintain the patrol boats, *speculatoria navigia*, were smaller than those of the Classis Britannia. They had steeper slips, but were functionally similar to their larger counterparts. These boathouses were also probably timber framed, weatherboarded and thatched, storing equipment and sails as well as the boats themselves.

Angles, Saxons, Frisians and Jutes

Norsemen from Denmark and north Germany raided southern and eastern Britain from the fourth century. By the mid-fifth century, when Britain had ceased to be a Roman province, piracy turned to settlement. The importance of seagoing ships to the Saxons is evident from ship burials in Suffolk at Sutton Hoo and Snape. The Sutton Hoo ship, clinker built and made of oak strakes with a 'keel-plank', was ideally suited for coast and river but dependent on seasonal repair.

The boathouses, where the ships were dried, repaired and re-caulked in England, doubtless reflected those in their Saxon homeland: timber buildings, possibly with supporting stone walls and thatched roofs. They are described in north German documents from the eighth to twelfth centuries.

One of the covered boathouses at the Slav trading area of Ralswick on the island of Rügen in the Baltic has been excavated revealing its wooden structure. In Frankish Salic law, the word *ascus* is used for a boat sufficiently valuable to be kept under lock and key. Theft incurred a punitive fine.

Vikings

In AD 789, three ships landed at Portland. The Vikings on board were mistaken for traders and they killed the reeves who were to take them to the king. Four years later Viking raiders sacked Lindisfarne Abbey. Norse raiding soon led to settlement and the Anglo-Saxon Chronicle later describes how Danish raiders – many of them now settled in England – used fast, manoeuvrable *askars*, built 'many years before'. Some were drawn up on the dunes, while others were stored in boathouses between raids.

Raiding continued as the Norse sailed against Northumbria, Orkney and Shetland. Settlement led to the destruction of the kingdom of Northumbria, creation of the kingdom of York and establishment of the Danelaw in eastern England. Further west the Norse seized the western isles, the Isle of Man and founded the trading centres of Dublin and Wexford. Boathouses, *nausts*, were an integral part of Norse culture. Nearly 850 have been recognised in Scandinavia and Scotland. Most were built for a single boat, their open gable facing the sea above high water.

Each boathouse had a landing place (*stø*), slipway (*opptrekk*) and timber floor. They originated in the third century AD and were associated with warships as well as fishing, hunting and collecting eider down. Typically, these boathouses are 20–40 metres long and 3–7 metres wide. Timber framed, sometimes with thatched roofs, their sides were protected

Viking settlement with a *naust* (boathouse), based on the settlement at Bork, Denmark. The ship was a key part of Norse life and this settlement is typical of those recorded on Orkney and Shetland. (Ian Robert Davis)

by piled stones. The larger *naust* and the smaller *hrof* were the most important boat-related constructions of the time – signifiers of social cohesion and often built in clusters. The *naust* was a place for boat maintenance, feasting and shelter. Inside, pottery and other debris suggests they were occupied during the summer when the longships were at sea.

In Norway, boathouses were associated with large burial mounds, long houses, halls and ring-shaped court sites. These were centres of power which combined chieftain farms with military organisation. Places of assembly, they reflected ethnic interaction when a longship was launched or repaired. Crushed pottery found in the boathouses may be the remains of ritual offerings to the gods. During the summer, these large boathouses could be used as feasting halls when the king arrived with all his followers. The sagas describe the coronation of the Norwegian King Haakon Haakonson in 1271 when he was crowned in a large boathouse at Avaldsnes.

In Britain, *nausts* have been recorded on the mainland and Shetland but are best known on Orkney where they have been identified on North Ronaldsay, Mainland and Brough of Birsay. On Papa Westray, *nausts* are known at Whitehowe and Binnaskirk, place names suggesting trading, farms and *skennist* where warships were laid up for the winter. Boathouses remained important components in Norse settlements into the eleventh century and their structure is reflected in 'hogbacks', grave markers which represent the built structures of the Viking world. They communicated a sense of origin and identity for the Viking diaspora.

Viking boathouse, or *naust*, based on a reconstruction at Bukkøy, Avaldsnes, Norway. A busy focus where Viking longboats were repaired, loaded with trade goods or embarked on raids to the west. Boathouses of this type have been identified in Scotland, north-west England and Ireland. (Ian Robert Davis)

Viking tombstones at St Mary's Church, Gosforth, Newcastle upon Tyne. The rear stone is known as the 'Saint's Tomb' and the front the 'Warriors Tomb'. Both were found under the church wall in 1896–97. The stones mimic Viking buildings, including boathouses, and gave a sense of origin and identity for the Viking diaspora. (Brian Deegan)

In England, the reign of Edward the Confessor (1042–66) was dubbed by naval historian N. A. M. Roger 'the golden age of the Anglo-Saxon navy'. The fleet served with the army and if needed for long periods it returned to port to change crews. The English naval base was London, and most ships were laid-up for winter. It is likely that above London Bridge there were boathouses similar to the Viking *nausts*. It made sense to protect an expensive warship from inevitable decay rather than expose it to winter conditions hauled up on a beach. The boathouse was a key component and although churches in Scandinavia may have been used to store sails when navies were raised by ship-muster, the boathouse in England was probably a familiar feature of many estuaries and early coastal ports.

2

Safeguard of the Sea: Navy and Coastguard

Later medieval boathouses were practical buildings. They provided protection for ships and boats over winter and, with the increasing size of warships in the sixteenth century, doubled up as workshops where small boats that serviced the men-o'-war were built.

Late Medieval Naval Boathouses

After the Norman Conquest in 1066 military power shifted to reliance on a land-based army and by the twelfth century naval operations were largely a matter of transport. The cog, a shell-built boat, became the essential cargo carrier, but oared galleys remained the most valuable warships. Manoeuvrable, fast and ideal for amphibious warfare in coastal waters, they were the vessel of choice for English kings. Their light oak hulls, though, deteriorated if left afloat so it was essential to build costly docks and boathouses to maintain them. Medieval boathouses are often referred to as 'covered slips'. King John's (r. 1199–1216) fleet, divided into four, was kept in massive stone shelters at Portsmouth, Southampton, Rye and Winchelsea. These may have been dismantled by the time Henry III (r. 1216–72) ordered covered 'ship-houses' or 'galley houses' wide enough for two ships to be built at Winchelsea in 1237. At the same time, records show there were boathouses for seven galleys at Rye with more at Chester, Bristol and Dunwich.

Longships, expensive to build, were still deployed during the reign of Henry VIII. Among the Tudor navy of the 1540s was the Mediterranean-designed *Galley Subtle*, but ships such as the *Mary Rose* could be repaired by careening. It meant there was less need for large boathouses. Both Henry VII (r. 1485–1509) and Henry VIII (r. 1509–47) saw a permanent navy as a symbol of royal power and by the start of the Seven Years War (1756–63) the Royal Navy was operating on a global scale. Pressure to support the fleet was intense and by the eighteeth century the Admiralty under Lord Anson was instrumental in systematically improving the nation's dockyards.

The great rebuilding between 1760 and 1808 was an important period of innovation. From at least the fourteenth century warships carried three boats, and inventories refer to a grete bote, a cokkebote and a jollyavatt. These were built in boathouses, when advancing maritime technology and the increasing size and complexity of modern warships placed even greater emphasis on the boats needed to support a man-o'-war. At Plymouth in 1769 among the hemp houses, seasoning sheds and mast houses, a long boathouse adjacent to the boat pool was where the barges, pinnaces, shallops, wherrys and cutters were built and maintained. Plans for the enlargement of Portsmouth in 1786 show the earlier rectangular 'Boat Store House' and a 'Boat House' of twenty-four bays in the centre of the yard. The new layout relocated the boat store houses next to the boat pond closer to a narrow channel to the sea, while the new boat store house had nine boat bays and workshops where boats were built, opening onto the boat pond.

Boathouses were a small but important part of the naval establishment. Their plans reflect the functionality, innovation and the regularity of Georgian 'rational architecture'. At Portsmouth, their design was the responsibility of the master shipwright who was answerable to the Navy Board in London.

The earliest surviving naval boathouses are at Portsmouth, Chatham and Sheerness. At Portsmouth, new boathouses dating from the mid-1800s reflect changes in technology. No. 6, built in brick in 1845, has a cast-iron frame supporting a second floor, designed by Lieutenant Roger Beatson. It makes 'dramatic use of cast iron' but was massively over specified. The floor supports were able to take some 40 tons – far beyond the needs of small boat maintenance. It has been described as a 'structural engineering blind alley'. More importantly, it lacked open working space so that by 1857 the deputy director of works described it as 'totally unsuited either for a working boathouse or boatstore'. Nevertheless, it remained in service until 1980.

Two single-storey boathouses built in 1872 (No. 7) and 1882 (No. 5) were originally mast houses, two storeys high with a loft above, and both overlie the mast pond. Together

Boathouse No. 6, Portsmouth Naval Dockyard. Built of brick in 1845, this boathouse was massively over specified. The three portals open onto slips into the mast pond and miniport, which was dug out in 1665 by soldiers and Dutch prisoners of war. (Elliott Brown)

Portsmouth Boathouse No. 5, Portsmouth Historic Dockyard. Originally a sail store, it was turned into a boathouse where the boats servicing the great nineteenth-century men-o'-war were built and maintained. (The wub)

with the 'Lower Boat House' at Chatham, these are the last surviving examples of a once common building type. At Chatham, the lower boathouse dates to 1844 and is a two-storey wooden-clad building, listed as a 'boat store'. Charles Dickens walked there:

> ... among the quiet lofts of stores – of sails, spars, rigging, ships' boats – determined to believe that somebody in authority wears a girdle and bends beneath the weight of a massive bunch of keys, and that, when such a thing is wanted, he comes telling his keys like Blue Beard, and opens such a door.

In contrast, the Sheerness boathouse, which was built in 1858, was a revolutionary design by Colonel G. T. Green, Royal Engineers. The design, influenced by larger ship sheds that covered the slips at Portsmouth and Chatham, was the 'first multi-floored, metal framed building'. It was the forerunner of multistorey iron-framed buildings worldwide and has become an icon in construction history.

The boatsheds at Portsmouth remained in service throughout the First World War. In the Second World War, No. 6 was damaged. No. 4 was built during the rearmament drive at the start of the war and commissioned in 1939. A four-storey industrial shed, it played an important part in preparations for D-Day and was where the experimental X4 midget submarines were built. These were the prototypes of operational craft which damaged the German pocket battleship *Tirpitz* in 1943. Boathouse No. 4 was the last naval boathouse built in Britain and today is part of the Portsmouth Historic Dockyard. Modern naval workboats are built and maintained by commercial yards such as those at Safehaven in Ireland or assembled by AEUK's Winfrith facility in Dorset, with testing on the Bincleaves Range in Portland Harbour.

Boathouse No. 4 was finished in 1939. It played a part in preparations for D-Day. It was where X4 midget submarines, prototypes of operational submarines that damaged the German battleship *Tirpitz* in 1943. It was the last boathouse built for the navy in Britain and is part of the Portsmouth Historic Dockyard. (Shutterstock)

Coastguard

While the navy operated deep sea, coastal waters were the preserve of the coastguard. It was here that boathouses contributed to the battle against smugglers. In 1749, the Duke of Richmond described how: 'The smugglers had reigned a long time uncontrolled; the officers of the customs were too few to encounter them; they rode in troops to fetch their goods and carried them off in triumph in daylight.' Smuggling was endemic in the sixteenth century and fortunes were made from tea, wool, fabrics, brandy and gin. Customs and excise duties were so high that at sea and on land gangs operated countrywide. The most intense activity was in Kent and Essex from where a fast-rowing boat could reach the French coast in five hours. Cargo ships anchored offshore were unloaded by the smugglers in small boats. Challenge by the Preventive Water Guard, Riding Officers or Revenue Cruisers could be fatal, and by 1746 the penalty for smuggling was hanging.

To counter the violence early boathouses provided shelter for the rowing boats and gigs of the inshore patrols. They were built where smugglers operated and one of the earliest survivals is at Pier Road, Seaview, on the Isle of Wight, dated 1557. It was built during the reign of Queen Mary (1553–58) whose new Book of Rates allowed the government to tax imports after the disastrous fiscal effects of Henry VIII's wars with France.

In the eighteenth century, the Board of Customs had a small number of cutters which operated close inshore. They were supported by patrols on land. Ratings based at watch stations patrolled nightly along the coast under the command of a 'boatsitter'. The boats were kept in boathouses like that at Wembury, Plymouth, a stone-built, slate-roofed, strictly functional building intended to protect a small patrol boat. A wide doorway opens onto a stone-surfaced slipway, giving easy access to the River Yelm; a boat launched from here could 'rummage' incoming cargoes, train new recruits and spot smuggling gangs at sea.

Old Boathouse, Seaview, Isle of Wight. Built in 1557, it was restored in around 1840/50. The ornamental barge boards and yellow brick Jacobean chimney are all nineteenth century. Jimi Hendrix stayed here when performing at the 1970 Isle of Wight Festival. (Alamy)

Polperro was the first place to which men of the newly organised Preventive Watch Guard were sent in 1800. Here the old watch house had a boathouse on the ground floor immediately adjacent to the harbour. The local smugglers were organised by the notorious Zephaniah Job, a financier known as the 'Smugglers Banker', who had moved to the port around 1770. The watch house was deliberately sited on the quayside to intimidate the smugglers, and a similar approach was adopted at Brixham, where the watch house with a boat bay in the basement was built on the Kings Quay.

In 1822, the coastguard service was formally established and in 1831, taking over from the Coast Blockade under the Board of Customs, the entire coastline came under its supervision. The Admiralty appointed coastguard officers and effectively created a naval reserve. Initially based in sixty-five ports, boathouses such as that at Berwick became essential in keeping the inshore patrols at sea. Here the boathouse, a later addition to the watch house built in the late eighteenth century, was ideally placed to challenge incoming shipping and launch river patrols.

In 1856, the Coastguard Service Act permitted the service to buy land, and by 1879 there were 314 stations. Boathouses were now the hub of a larger complex with housing for staff, and watch rooms or cart sheds for life-saving equipment. The 'boathouse was home to a stout pinnace or yawl, ready for any work that may be necessary'. Increasingly effective against smuggling, the service became progressively responsible for wrecks and ships in distress.

With wider responsibilities and more stations, the service still maintained close links with local landowners. At Budleigh Salterton, south-east of Exeter, eight two-storey coastguard cottages linked by steps to a boathouse were built in 1873 on land owned by Lord Rolle. Although the plans were drawn up by the Devonport architect John Haite, they were approved by Rip Lipscomb, steward to the landowner.

The standardised design is still evident in many places. At King's Lynn five cottages and an officer's house also included a boathouse, built in 1883, and at East Cowes the coastguard station, built in 1882, similarly comprises a terrace of cottages with two boathouses adjacent to the officer's quarters. Here the architecture, an angular Gothic, was clearly intended to emphasise the status of the service.

The Old Watch House and boathouse at Polperro, built in the late eighteenth century for the coastguard. It was intended to intimidate the smugglers when tea, gin, brandy and tobacco were smuggled through the tiny port into Cornwall from Guernsey. (Jo and Steve Turner)

Burgh Head on the Moray Firth was established as a lookout and coastguard station in the early nineteenth century. Located on a prominent site overlooking harbour and Burghead Bay, the boathouse and store were added in 1860. (Shutterstock)

The coastguard boathouse and station at Dawlish in Devon. The boathouse was designed in the 1840s by Isambard Kingdom Brunel. When the South Devon Railway was built between the cliff and the beach, the watch house was moved to the other side of the railway. The boathouse was demolished after storm damage in 2014. (Shutterstock)

At the outbreak of the First World War most coastguard officers were called up. After the war, its life-saving function reduced, the service was reorganised under the Board of Trade. Many stations were closed down. Further reorganisation after 1974 saw the remaining accommodation sold off to leave a slimmed-down service with no requirement for boathouses.

Coastguard watch house and boathouse on Lepe Beach, built in 1828. The boathouse was taken over by the military during the Second World War. The beach was site of the PLUTO pipeline to Normandy, where Mulberry harbour units were made and troops embarked for D-Day. (Jim Champion)

3

For Those in Peril on the Sea

From the late eighteenth century lifeboat houses have reflected changing economic and leisure priorities along the British coastline. The coast was a treacherous place in the age of sail. Prevailing westerlies, rocky shores and shallow, shifting sandbanks meant shipwrecks were common. Before the eighteenth century rescues were rare. The Great Storm of 1703 was devastating, with numerous shipwrecks, including several Royal Navy warships, and the lives of nearly 8,000 sailors lost. With the expansion of the British Empire came high volumes of coastal trade and an increasing number of losses. In 1782, the *Royal George*, a first-rate ship of the line, capsized off Spithead, Portsmouth, during routine maintenance. Over 800 people died including women and children visiting the ship.

Pilots and lightermen were the earliest lifesavers, but the first formal designation of a lifeboat was at Formby in the 1770s, followed by another at Hoylake, both established by the Liverpool Docks Commission. In the North East, the dangers to shipping led to competition to build an effective lifeboat and by the end of the century the boatbuilder Henry Greathead (1757–1818) was described as the 'inventor of the lifeboat'.

Aldborough. The former lifeboat house combines the north lookout tower built for the pilot in 1850. This was built together with a small gig shed in competition with a south pilot and lookout. The lifeboat house, with the red doors, was added in the twentieth century.

Lifeboat Houses

Early lifeboats were often drawn up on the beach, but very soon the lifeboat house became the principal building of a lifeboat station. It housed the boat, its equipment, oars, sails, spars and masts and cart.

One of the earliest was at Redcar, paid for by Lord Dundas, a local landowner. He had lost a sloop off Redcar in February 1802 and funding the lifeboat was in response to the loss of his crew. The boathouse, 9 × 3 metres, was designed to take the *Zetland* lifeboat. It was 300 yards from the sea and not only stored the lifeboat and its equipment but also a supply of logs. When the lifeboat was launched from land closest to the wreck the logs were used to form a railway-like track across soft sand, the concave wheels of the carriage engaging with the timber to get the lifeboat into position. Despite its distance from the sea, the boathouse was vulnerable to the weather. When a storm drove local fishing cobles aground in 1824, an anonymous correspondent in the *Newcastle Chronicle* blamed the lifeboatmen for the loss of seven lives because they were too slow to clear the sand that had blocked the lifeboat-house doors.

Many early lifeboats were moored without boathouses or maintained by the coastguard, but in 1824 increasing losses led to the foundation of the Royal National Institute for the Preservation of Life from Shipwreck (RNIPLS). There was still no co-ordinated approach to the location of lifeboat stations and arrangements were often ad hoc. The first Padstow lifeboat, for instance, was kept on the quayside, while the St Ives lifeboat was kept in a fish cellar next to the coastguard boathouse on the beach: 'In the early days of the RNLI [Royal National Lifeboat Institution], when expense was a primary consideration the houses in which its lifeboats were kept were ... little better than sheds', complained a review in the trade journal *Builder* in 1883. Not all the early lifeboat houses were as insubstantial as the *Builder* implies. At Appledore the first lifeboat was housed in the Kings Watch House, overlooking the estuary until 1831 when the North Devon Humane Society had a large stone boathouse built. It housed two lifeboats which served Bideford Bay. At St Mary's, Isles of Scilly, the coastguard was associated with lifesaving and raised £26 19*s* 6*d* for a stone-built lifeboat house on the beach at Hugh Town, run by the RNIPLS.

The early boathouses reflected the local vernacular, familiar in villages and farms where robust, generally rectangular buildings provided shelter for equipment and livestock. In the 1840s, fundraising faltered, but the loss of a lifeboat and twenty lives in sight of land at South Shields in 1849 gripped the public imagination. As interest in the lifeboats rose, so did the impetus for change. A report by the Lifeboat Commissioners in 1850 advocated the creation of local committees and set out the principles on which stations should operate. It included a requirement that a boathouse should have three keys: one held by the coxswain, the others assigned at the discretion of the local committee.

Significantly, Richard Lewis, journalist and parliamentary reporter, was appointed secretary in 1850 and in 1851 the Duke of Northumberland elected president. They formed a dynamic partnership, searching for an improved lifeboat and setting in train a review which led to the creation of the RNLI in 1854. It became the sole organisation providing lifeboats at national level, taking over from the coastguard and the Shipwrecked Fishermen and Mariners Royal Benevolent Society.

Mid-century was a period of renewal. Organisational changes led to an increase in lifeboat houses from ninety-six in 1850 to 242 in 1874. From 1850 boathouse design was dominated by the RNLI's architect, Charles H. Cooke FSA (1829–88). Well-known for the Godolphin School, Hammersmith, built in the 1860s, and the restoration of the Church of St Nicholas, Plumstead, in 1867–68, Cook designed nearly 300 lifeboat houses. The *Builder* described how:

> as its stations multiplied it was ... desirable not only to provide lifeboat houses of larger size and ... a more complete and tenable character ... but ... to give them a more or less ornamental or ... seemly exterior ... especially in cases where legacies or donations of large amounts had been given to the institute to provide a complete lifeboat establishment.

The Walmer lifeboat house, illustrated in the *Builder,* 1875. In that year the lifeboats had saved 543 lives, and twelve new lifeboat houses had been built the year before.

Walmer lifeboat house in April 2012. The boathouse was extended to accommodate larger modern lifeboats. (Stephen Craven)

Cooke's designs, inspired by contemporary ecclesiastical architecture, captured the evangelical spirit of the RNLI and gave his boathouses their distinctive chapel-like character. Common features included large doorways at the front for boat and carriage, a lookout window from a loft above the main entrance, and sometimes, like those at Hastings and Hornsea, a watch or bell tower to summon the crew.

Unlike the coastguard, the RNLI's boathouses did not include accommodation as the crews were local seamen. The new boathouses were located where there was a high incidence of wrecks, sufficient local workforce to raise a crew and the local community could be expected to raise the £300–400 necessary for a boathouse and maintain the station.

Clacton-on-Sea, illustrated in the *Builder* on 15 September 1883. Built in 1883, the boathouse remained in service until it was replaced in 1929. Today it is a pub, described by Pevsner as 'lacking its original charm'.

The chapel-like lifeboat house at Hastings was built at the eastern end of the Marine Parade at a cost of £650 in 1882. It replaced an earlier boathouse at Rock-a-Nore, constructed by local builder Edwin Harman in 1852. The boathouse was demolished in 1959.

The lifeboat station at Runswick Bay was established in 1875 but closed in 1922 due to the decline of fishing and the shortage of crewmen. When new breakwaters and harbour were built, the fishing industry revived and in 1928 the station reopened. It closed again in 1938 but re-opened in 1978 and was renamed Staithes and Runswick. (habiloid)

Funding at a national level was subsidised by the Board of Trade but the service relied on local initiatives. Disaster was often associated with personal philanthropy. At Polperro, on the southern tip of the Lizard, the steamship *Czar* hit the Vogue Rock and sank with the loss of thirteen lives. Brought to the attention of Agar Roberts and his mother, they provided £269 for a boathouse and lifeboat in 1859. In the same year, the loss of the schooner *Endeavour* led the Rashleigh family, landowners of the Menabilly estate in Cornwall, to contribute, land, money and materials to build the lifeboat house at Polkerris. At Hastings in 1882, Charles Arkoll, owner of the Lion Brewery at Chatham, paid for the boathouse in memory of his late father.

Institutional donors were equally important. The Freemasons contributed to the boathouse at Hope Cove, on Bigbury Bay, Devon, completed in 1878 on a site given by the Earl of Devon. The boathouse symbolised the Masonic principle of promoting mutual help in times of distress. It was one of a pair. At Clacton-on-Sea, Essex, the Freemasons donated £600 for boat and boathouse to celebrate the safe return from India of the Grand Master, the Prince of Wales. The procession in full Masonic honours reinforced the Masons' alignment with the monarchy and promoted their status as more than a prosperous social club.

In the north several benefactors were industrialists whose business and social conscience aligned with safety at sea. At Lytham St Annes, a lifeboat house was constructed in 1881 with funds donated by James Chadwick of High Bank, Prestwich, who owned mills in Canada, America and Lithuania.

The principles behind boathouse design were convenience, durability and ventilation. They were built to house particular lifeboats, their designs changing as lifeboats improved. At Clovelly, the boathouse constructed in 1870 housed the 33-foot, ten-oared *Alexander and*

Matilda Boattefeur. In 1892, it was rebuilt with a new slipway to house the 34-foot *Elinor Roget.* Finally, in 1999, it was extended to accommodate the inflatable Atlantic 75 class lifeboat and its launching tractor.

Not all lifeboat houses were near the water's edge. The first boathouse at the Lizard was built at the top of the cliff above Polpeor Cove in 1914. At Port Isaac the lifeboat had to be hauled manually through the winding streets to a boathouse at the top of the village.

By the end of the century many boathouses were old. A letter to the *Redcar and Saltburn News* on 28 January 1893 stated that the *Zetland* lifeboat was to be retired and put on display but not in the 'rickety old building', which had been its shelter for many years. By 1895 there were 308 lifeboat houses. The influence of contemporary industrial design, new materials and a more functional approach meant radical design changes. At Cromer the lifeboat, kept on the east jetty from 1804, was in poor condition by 1857 and a lifeboat house was built above the high-water mark. The RNLI maintained the station but by 1868

Exmouth lifeboat house, built in 1903. The first boathouse was washed away in a storm in 1814. Another boathouse was built near the beach but replaced in 1903 on the same site. From 1961 the lifeboat was kept afloat on the river and the boathouse retained as a display centre. From 1966 it housed an inshore lifeboat.

Minehead lifeboat house was built in 1901 west of the pier at a cost of £785. In 1993, the front and side were extended to improve crew facilities and provide a souvenir sales outlet as well as housing the inshore Atlantic 21 class lifeboat. (Lewis Clarke)

another was built when the sea walls were extended. It was paid for by Benjamin Cabbell of Cromer Hall, magistrate, Freemason and Conservative MP. This boathouse was replaced in 1902 and still survives as the Inshore Lifeboat Station, but in 1923 it was superseded by an even larger boathouse at the end of the pier. It was a functional, steel-framed, timber-clad structure designed by Henry Blogg, a long-serving coxswain of the lifeboat, and intended for the new motorised Norfolk and Suffolk class lifeboat and not replaced until 1999.

Post-war fashions and technology changed the focus of the RNLI. Accidents in the 1920s involving cross-Channel flights increased demand for high-speed, long-range rescue, while the rising popularity of seaside holidays increased the need for inshore lifesavers. With the advent of diesel and petrol engines several older lifeboat stations were closed.

The Second World War saw the RNLI taken under naval command and tensions arose as crews had to get consent from the navy to go to sea. On shore there was no new building work, but construction of coastal defences could be a problem. In Hastings contractors working on the beach defences in March 1943 had blocked access with building materials. It meant a delay of over two hours before the lifeboat could be launched to rescue the remaining crew on the HMS *Caulonia,* which had run aground off Rye Bay.

This lifeboat house was built in 1923 and once located at the end of Cromer pier. Today it houses a former Southwold lifeboat and is the Alfred Corry Museum at Southwold.

St Justinian's lifeboat station at St David's, Pembrokeshire. The original lifeboat house, to rear left, was built in 1869 and extensively repaired in 1890. The new boathouse (centre) was built in 1910 representing the new functional designs of the twentieth century. It was replaced in 2016. The original boathouse still operates as the base for a boarding boat. (Philip Halling)

Occasionally a boathouse was in the news for other reasons. At Wells-next-the-Sea, Norfolk, in 1946, German prisoners, anxious to return home after the Second World War, broke into the boathouse and attempted to steal the lifeboat, only failing because they could not start the engine.

By the 1960s inshore rescue was increasingly important, with seventy-two new inflatable boats on station to cope with the rising popularity of beach holidays and sailing. In some places, the new boats led to the reopening of older boathouses. New fundraising initiatives emerged, such as the *Blue Peter* television appeal which paid for a boathouse at St Agnes, Isles of Scilly. However, it was a period of mediocre design. The new boathouse at Newquay, for example, as described by Nicholas Leach, was a functional yet 'somewhat rudimentary building which offered little in the way of crew facilities and was typical of the boathouses used in the 1960s and 1970s'.

The late twentieth century saw the emergence of a new class of boathouse. Characteristic of these is the boathouse at Southwold on the River Blyth, Suffolk. Designed to store the Atlantic 21 lifeboat in 1993, it includes fuel store, crew facilities and derrick to launch the lifeboat. Similar state-of-the-art facilities can be seen at resorts such as Lyme Regis, where a new B class boathouse on the harbour wall was completed in 1997, and north Norfolk, where a modern station at Wells-next-the-Sea replaced the 1890s boathouse on the beach.

Pragmatism characterised the late twentieth century. When the pleasure boat *Marchioness* went down on the Thames in 1989 it exposed a gap in the provision for life-saving and led to an extension of RNLI responsibility upriver to Teddington Lock. A new boathouse, like a garage, was established in a block of flats. In the twenty-first century, boathouses home to a new generation of lifeboats and crews operate in an age when many are designed to reflect their surroundings rather than make a statement.

The new Lyme Regis lifeboat house. In 1991, the wealthy philanthropist Eugenie Boucher left £4 million to the RNLI who used the money build new stations. However, Lyme Regis became the focus of protest because of its impact on views of the Cobb before the design was finally approved.

Southwold lifeboat house on the River Blyth, Suffolk, was built in 1993. Since 2013 it has housed the Atlantic 85 class lifeboat *Annie Tranmer* and covers over 25 miles of coastline between Lowestoft and Aldeburgh.

Aldeburgh, Suffolk. The lifeboat station was built in 1994 replacing a smaller one on the same site. The new station houses the boat and Talus MB-H tractor. The design includes a public viewing platform, facilities for the crew and store. It was also built using part of the bequest of Mrs Eugenie Boucher.

4

Hunting, Shooting and Fishing: Celebrating the Vernacular

It was 1926 and the start of a great adventure in the Lake District for *Swallows and Amazons*: 'The boathouse was a stone one, with a narrow quay along each wall inside, and a small jetty sticking beyond it into the lake. Roger had got the door open by the time they came to it, though he had a tough struggle with the rusty lock.' Arthur Ransome was inspired by the boathouse at Lanehead on Coniston, one of many practical boathouses associated with farms and private houses. Typically, the Lakeland examples represent a local tradition, sited according to need rather than by design. Traditional attributes characterise boathouses associated with the everyday: fishing and duck hunting, boatyards and ferries, wetland management and boat hire. They are often short-lived, abandoned, dismantled or rebuilt, reflecting the inexpensive and readily available materials from which they are built.

These boathouses are seldom seen in the professional or commercial media. They rarely satisfy the criteria for designation as listed buildings or invite comments in architectural reviews. Despite this, timeworn practical boathouses have a beauty of their own and occupy a significant niche in the art world of painting and photography.

Fishing, Ferries and Wildfowling

The earliest references to practical boathouses are associated with fishponds on the great ecclesiastical estates of medieval England. One of the best known is that of the Bishop of Winchester, who in the thirteenth century held lands between Farnham, Portsmouth and Southampton.

Fishponds, *vivaria,* were a source of food and their management a complex process of breeding, fishing and maintenance. Some, like Frensham Great Pond, near Farnham in Surrey, were over 100 acres and boats were essential for their management. Boathouses – where boats were built, repaired and maintained – were an important resource. Most *vivaria* had their own fishing boats and there may have been a boat-building yard at

Bishops Waltham. In 1220, records show an old boat was mended, two boats were newly made and a boathouse (*domus ad botellos*) was built there. As late as 1785 a boathouse is shown on a bank between the fishpond and the palace.

No medieval boathouses relating to fishing survive. A replica of the post-medieval fisher's Chepstow boathouse, dismantled in the 1940s, is preserved in the St Fagans National Museum of History in Cardiff. It was open-fronted and wooden-framed with weatherboarded sides and a pantile roof, and had acted as workshops for the fishermen of the Wye estuary. It stored the putcher (cone-shaped woven willow traps), stop net (bag-like nets suspended from two heavy poles) and drift nets (a wall-like net shot from a boat across the current) as well as the fisher's bowl-shaped coracles.

In the east, as early as 1548, the company of fishermen complained to Norwich Corporation that the Broads were being overfished. Using nets or eel sets, boats were essential and boathouses important in protecting the marshman's double-ended punts. The earliest visual representation of a Broads boathouse is by P. H. Emerson. Preeminent among photographers, he captured the boathouse form in the well-known *A Reed Boat-House*. In 1886–87, it was almost certainly the home of a marshman's lighter, used for fishing or reed harvesting.

Chepstow boathouse is now reconstructed in the St Fagans National Museum of History. The original was on the River Wye until the 1940s. In addition to the legitimate nets and fishing equipment, it also contained otter boards, treble hooks and salmon spears used in salmon poaching. (Alamy)

A reed boathouse on the Norfolk Broads, photographed by P. H. Emerson in 1886. Boathouses of this type housed the punts and small wherries used by the marshmen when collecting reeds, fishing or hunting.

Place names suggest similar patterns elsewhere. Between the rivers Alt and Douglas near Ormskirk, Lancashire, is an area once exploited for its fishing, reeds and grazing. On the fringe of Martin Mere, drained in 1697, Boathouse Field in Burscough suggests a boathouse on sandy soil beside the mere where boats were used to drive cattle, harvest reeds or for fishing. In Staffordshire, Boathouse Wood suggests the location of another historic boathouse on Aqualate Mere.

In Emerson's *The Fowlers Return* (1887), two wild fowlers land near their small boathouse, a simple thatched structure over a small wet bay. The fowlers exploited the rivers, hunting with shotguns from a marshman's punt. Several estates in the Broads created their own decoys which comprised a central open pond with curving dykes leading along a netted pipe where the ducks were trapped. Once they reached the point of no return, the birds were caught, and their necks rung. The decoys were managed by boat which in some cases were kept in boathouses on the edge of the decoy lake. Sir Ralph Payne Gallwey described how a boat could be concealed during the day in a 'boat harbour roofed with planks and turf'. An example survives today at Hale in Lancashire where among the brickwork is a stone dated 1633 with the initials 'R C'.

Eel fishers in the Norfolk Broads. Eel was a staple food until the 1940s. The traps baited with fish gut were weighted down with stones at either end and left in the river overnight to catch the eels as they swam upstream. The eel fishers depended on boats to set the traps and kept their punts in nearby makeshift boathouses. (Alamy)

A small reed-covered boathouse in the Norfolk Broads, from *The Fowlers Return*, photographed by P. H. Emerson in 1886. It shows two duck hunters and their makeshift boathouse.

Further north in the Lake District, the earliest boathouses date to the eighteenth century. Although boats were used as ferries, for fishing or carried cargoes such as slate, timber and bark, Adam Menuge at the National Trust has argued boathouses only emerged when boats were fitted out for pleasure. They were part of the country house tradition of hunting and fishing, plain stone structures with low eaves and slate roofs such as that on the Graythwaite estate, on the west shore of Windermere, or Dale End on Grasmere which remains substantially as built. On Ullswater the Hasel family had a boathouse from which their boat was used to ferry hunting parties between the house and their hunting lodge at Martindale. A boathouse of Charles Howard, Earl of Surrey, at Lyulphins Tower on Ullswater was on a grander scale. Boats were kept there to ferry tourists so they could enjoy one of the early 'characteristic' pastimes of the lakes, firearms discharged to experience the echoes reverberating around the surrounding mountains. The Duke of Portland's boathouse on Ullswater, now a holiday let, provided similar opportunities in the 1770s.

Probably the earliest riverbank boathouses were those associated with medieval ferry crossings. For example, in 1354 Adam Bibby leased land in Ribchester on the River Ribble to William de Bradley, ferryman. He was to hold the lease by paying 12*d* annual rent and ferrying men across the river. The ferryman was the occupant of Boathouse Farm, opposite Osbaldeston Hall. Although the ferry worked until 1903, there is no surviving boathouse. Downstream at Penwortham, another Boathouse Farm was part of the 1839 Tithe Apportionment, owned by Richard Breakell. In Scotland coastal ferries were essential among the islands and sea lochs and the remains of many early, rudimentary boathouses, or nausts, have been recorded along the shoreline above the high-water mark.

Naust and boathouse, Skeafea, Graemsay, Orkney. Looking across Burra Sound towards Ward Hill on Hoy. This rudimentary boathouse, *tigh bata* in Gaelic, was probably built by crofters in the early nineteenth century to house a fishing boat. (Claire Pegrum)

Cooper's Noust, Graemsay, Orkney. This ruined naust was probably built for fishing or a ferry boat during the nineteenth century and was protected by a thatched roof. The Graemsay ferry would go to a small pier at Cooper's Noust towards Hoy Low lighthouse. (Claire Pegrum)

Boatbuilding, Boat Hire and Maintenance

Boatsheds of the boatbuilding and boat-hire industry are beyond the scope of this brief introduction. Not only is it conventional to refer to 'sheds' but the scale of the buildings and nature of the industry has generated several books, podcasts and blogs which illustrate the industry's growth from fisher's sheds on the foreshore to the present-day industry. Nevertheless, a small proportion of companies and individuals work from premises described as 'boathouses'. These fall into the vernacular tradition, whether designed by an architect or put up by a local builder. Anyone cruising the rivers of the Norfolk Broads in the areas of Wroxham, Hickling or Hoveton will be familiar with the timber-built, thatched, canvas-covered or industrial-like sheds which flank the Broads and river courses. Boatsheds of Whispering Reeds, or historically those of Jack Powles, Ernest Collins or R. Moore & Son which were characteristic of the 1950s and 1960s, remain the focus of many local historians.

Like the nineteenth-century boathouses which appealed to Emerson, the colour and complexity of the modern vernacular boathouse has caught the imagination of contemporary artists. Paul Banning, John Bryce and Roy Glanville of the Wapping Group, for example, have all chosen to paint the boathouses of the lower Thames in oils and watercolour.

Boathouses specifically associated with boat maintenance are rarer. Often service boats are retained alongside other boating activities, such as the traditional timber launch *Bosporus* and the catamarans used for daily outings by the Oxford University Boat Club moored in the wet boathouse at Wallingford.

Occasionally a utilitarian boathouse is hidden away in a designed landscape such as that at Buscot Park, Oxfordshire. In the nineteenth century, Buscot was one of the most highly industrialised farms in England. Although many of the improvements by the owner, Robert Campbell, have now gone, the eighteenth-century lake and reservoirs he created remain. In 1904, Harold Peto laid out the Italianate water gardens for which the estate is famous. Hidden away to their north beside a hump-backed bridge over a canal is a small weatherboarded boathouse which houses the service boat for the 20-acre lake. It is a reminder of the discrete but important part boathouses play in contemporary landscape management.

Left: The Old Boathouse, Brentford, on the River Thames, by Paul Banning. A member of the Wapping group, his pictures capture the way the light falls and the changing nature of the river. (Paul Banning RI RSMA, paulbanning.com)

Below: Characteristic estuary boatsheds. These belong to the Harbour Marine Services, Southwold, Suffolk. The weatherboarded sheds reflect local practice alongside fisherman's huts and more recently artists' studios on the banks of the River Blyth.

A small weatherboarded boathouse with a pantile roof on the 20-acre lake at Buscot Park, Oxfordshire. The lake, created by Edward Loveden in the 1790s, was fed by a local stream and the boathouse is an essential part of its present-day maintenance.

5

From Barge Houses to Great Estates

In 1851, Henry Mayhew described how:

> … from the termination of the Wars of the Roses [1487] until the end of the 17th century … all the magnates of the metropolis, the king, the members of the royal family the great officers of state … the city companies and the Inns of court all kept their own or their state barges rowed by their servants … in the same way as carriages and horses are kept by them in our day.

Barge Houses

The earliest reference to a barge house is on the River Thames during the reign of Henry VI (r. 1422–61, 1470–71). By the sixteenth century, the royal Watergate at Hampton Court was a significant Tudor building. Built for Henry VIII (r. 1509–47), it was 'part landing stage, part bargehouse, part pleasure pavilion'. Not all barge houses were so grand. In 1550, after the Dissolution of the Monasteries, when the hospital of St Mary Rounceval at Charing Cross was granted to Sir Thomas Cawarden, it included a barge house. It was a functional wooden building straddling a stream, allowing a barge to dock with the rising tide.

View of Hampton Court Palace from the south with the River Watergate in the foreground by Anthonis van den Wyngaerde, 1558. The Watergate was built for Henry VIII and was described recently as 'part landing stage, part bargehouse, part pleasure pavilion'. (Alamy)

Royal palaces lined the Thames from Richmond to Greenwich under the Tudors. Whitehall was the home of the royal barge and where, in Scotland Yard, a long narrow dock was dug out. When a new barge was made in 1536 the dock was enlarged and a superstructure built over it to create a wet barge house. In 1593, the 'Royal Barge House' had been relocated to a south bank site on Upper Ground, at the western edge of Paris Gardens. Queen Elizabeth (r. 1558–1603) used her barge, which was kept just above Blackfriars Bridge near Barge House Alley, as a showpiece and a public stage for royal display. The barge house was timber framed, and even in the mid-twentieth century the oak pile foundations of the slipway could still be seen.

Under Charles I, the royal barge house was maintained by Edmund Chamers who was paid 20*s* in 1634. It fell into disrepair during the Civil War and in June 1652 it was described as 'a building of timber, covered with tile, 65 feet in length, and 26 feet in breadth; but much out of repair, and valued at *£8* per annum'. Meanwhile, the Right Honourable Counsell of State 'have ordered other bargehouses to be built for their use which are already finished'.

In 1656, during the Interregnum (1649–60), the Parliamentarian Thomas Scott petitioned John Thurloe, secretary to the Council of State and spymaster for Oliver Cromwell, to recover

The archbishop's boathouse at Lambeth, west of the palace (Kip, 1697). Narrow Wall, the old earth river wall, was probably the boundary between the archbishop's house and the river (now Lambeth Place Road). Here 'hopes' of land were reclaimed from the river in the area known as Bishop's Walk until the Albert Embankment was built. In the seventeenth and eighteenth centuries, the foreshore was mainly occupied by barge houses.

five or six years' rent for barge houses. It was a plea made urgent by his 'improvident sonne in France' whose wife had sent his daughter home for Scott to look after.

After the Restoration in 1660, Charles II (r. 1660–85) leased the King's Old Barge House site to John Arundel. Comprising 'three new barge houses ... with a little cottage belonging to one of them, together with free access down to the low water mark of the river of Thames', Arundel petitioned James II (1685–88) to continue the lease, which was in the manor of Kennington. It included Prince's Meadow and a ruined building called the King's Old Barge House, together with 'three edifices for boats called barge houses, the first ... in the use of the Mayor of London, the second with a little cottage in the use of the Merchant Taylors' Company ... and the third in the use of the Woodmongers' Company'.

The inauguration of the Lord Mayor of the City of London, which took place at Westminster until 1832, was celebrated annually by the great twelve city livery companies, craft or trade associations, originally medieval guilds of the City of London who processed upriver in their ceremonial barges. In 1693, the City recorded rent owed for the City barge house in a lease extended in 1697, and during the late seventeenth and eighteenth centuries Lambeth Reach was occupied by several barge houses, including those of the Armourers and Barber Surgeons. The Surgeons' barge house was built by Henry Fforty, while the Goldsmiths shared a large barge house with the Skinners, although both moved to land belonging to the Apothecaries at Chelsea in 1656. The Haberdashers rented their barge house for £4 per annum, sharing with the Pewterers in 1662. The Coopers and Vintners both rented in Lambeth before moving to Chelsea in 1739.

The City of London Barge House at Lambeth. The land around Old Barge House Stairs was part of Lambeth Marsh, an area of land between Lambeth and Blackfriars Bridges. It was the site of the King's Barge House, along with accommodation for the royal bargemaster under Henry VIII. (Alamy)

Queen Anne (1702–14) frequently used her barge, which was kept at Windsor. The queen was married to Prince George of Denmark and when the royal barge houses in Lambeth were damaged during the Great Storm of 1703, the 'Prince's bargehouses' had to be repaired. Two of them at Lambeth were leased by the bargemaster in June 1716, on behalf George I, but by February 1729 they were in a ruinous state. If the royal barge houses were not repaired quickly, 'they would be spoiled by the weather'. Ultimately, they were repaired and remained in use until at least 1808.

Barge-house design remained unchanged from the timber buildings with tiled roofs of 1652 until the mid-nineteenth century. By this time barges were going out of fashion. George IV had three barges when opening the New London Bridge in 1822, but by 1814 the Royal Barge House was already described as 'Old', and construction of Bishops Walk had severed Lambeth Palace from the river. When Samuel Leigh published the *Panorama of the Thames* in 1829 there were only four royal or aristocratic barge houses left.

Queen Victoria rarely travelled by barge, making an exception to open the new Coal Exchange in 1849, after which the boat was laid up in dry dock at Deptford. A new barge was built for the queen in 1884–85 but kept at Virginia Water, in Windsor Great Park, until 1936. The old Royal Barge House was subsequently used by James Messenger, the royal bargemaster from 1862, and occupied by the boatbuilders Porter and Brice between 1895 and 1910, before becoming the headquarters of the British Motor Yacht Club.

An Aristocratic Tradition

Boats, barges and state barges were an essential means of transport, especially among society who spent half the year in the metropolis. The dukes of Richmond and Montagu, who had houses across the river at Whitehall, had kept theirs on the Lambeth shore. A letter in 1694 to Mr Travers, Surveyor General of Crown Lands, recorded leases taken by William III (r. 1689–1702) on barge houses belonging to the Archbishop of Canterbury. Even so, it was not until 1699 that the Treasury recorded the payment of nine years' rent arrears.

Many society families had sons in the navy, and it was these families whose country estates were transformed in the 1730s from the formality of the Restoration and the Anglo-Dutch gardens of William and Mary into English landscape parks. The connection with the Thames was explicit. At Stowe, a barge commissioned by Lord Cobham was inspired by Prince Frederick's royal barge, and as his estate in Buckinghamshire was transformed during the 1740s a vaulted boathouse was built as part of the cascade separating the Octagon from the 11-acre lake. It was an integral part of the landscape garden, a neo-classical structure in a Grecian valley.

The landscapes of the mid-eighteenth century were not only intellectual pursuits and indicators of status and taste, but an opportunity for landowners to indulge in mock-naval battles, *naumachia*, and to entertain friends and guests with fishing and boating. Boathouses for sailing skiffs or rowing boats were part of the landscape. At Enville Hall, in Staffordshire, the boathouse on Temple Pool, built in 1769, had space for a small yacht and a room for entertainment. It was one of a series of picturesque buildings designed by Sanderson Miller, the pioneering Gothic architect, and visible in views across the lake towards the Welsh mountains.

Boathouse at Enville Hall, designed by Sanderson Miller and built in 1769. It replaced a Chinese temple at the north-east corner of the pool. In about 1970, a tree fell on it, and only a pile of rubble and stone blocks now remain. (Permission of Mrs Diana Williams, Enville Hall)

Enville is also one of the few boathouses described by visitors. Joseph Heely, a manufacturer of ironmongery from nearby Moseley Hall, recorded how in 1777: 'you came upon it unexpectedly ... an octagon, prettily ornamented within by festoons of flowers, and medallions in stucco. A curious sliding window, that opens to the water, adorned with painted glass in whimsical groups of grotesque figures'. William Marshall, in 1801, thought it:

> ... a romantic, almost fairytale building. Visitors to the Boathouse were brought inside, and while they were admiring the glass window a servant was sent to release the water held back by a dam and sluices above the cascades on the opposite side of the Pool. The window was then flung open, revealing the cascade as it entered the Pool in full flow and fury; foaming and bellowing, as if the mountain were enraged, pouring down a river of water as white as snow, and apparently so copious, as to render our situation alarming; less the house and its contents be hurried away with the torrent.

Views were carefully designed. The boathouse at Redgrave Hall in Suffolk, built *c.* 1766–70, was part of the landscape designed by Capability Brown and intended as an eye-catcher from the hall. To enhance the effect, it was built of white brick and flint with a black glazed pantile roof. Occasionally the eye-catcher may have been wrongly sited. In Capability Brown's landscape at Wotton, the Octagon provides views towards the boathouse but focuses on a mound which adds nothing to the garden, suggesting the boathouse 60 metres away may have been built in the wrong place.

Boathouse designs varied from the simple timber shelter on the lake at Buckland House, Oxfordshire, of 1750, to the elaborate design at Enville. The picturesque impact of the boathouse at Petworth, with its double portals, part of the Brown landscape of 1756, was captured in 1810 by J. M. W. Turner, but the high point is the boathouse at Kedleston, designed in 1769 by Robert Adam and built in 1771–72. Flanked by flower gardens, it combines a fishing and entertaining room over two vaulted boat bays.

Often practicality and aesthetics worked together. At Chillington Park, Staffordshire, the boathouse was built of brick with an open pediment framing the arched entrance and originally housed a boat for the journey by canal to the lake in the parkland. Capability Brown's landscapes were directly inspired by the paintings of Claude Lorraine and boathouses played a key role in many of his designed views. At Sharpham House in the Dart valley, the dramatic view of the Octagonal boathouse upstream epitomises the sublime. The view instils a sense of awe in the observer and almost immediately a pleasurable horror that what can be seen is not in fact natural.

At the end of the eighteenth century the Kedleston boathouse represented the apogee of boathouse design. It combined the practicality of the boat bays, the sociability of a fishing room and a cold plunge with the aesthetic qualities of a Classical landscape. Repton's boathouse at Hooton Park in Cheshire followed the same tradition with hot or cold, fresh, or salt water, in a bath tended by a keeper whose lodge was to be close by. Boathouses were more than just aesthetic additions to a garden as the office of water porter in Repton's other proposals at Stowe, Virginia Water and Holkham suggests. At Kedleston the card table in the inventory and proposals shown in Basset's Plan of 1788 for a boathouse with banqueting room in Windsor Great Park add entertaining to the boathouse repertoire.

The boathouse in Wollaton Park, Nottingham, was designed to catch the eye and look like a bridge when seen from the hall. The estate lake was made in 1774–85, but today the water level has been reduced, leaving the boathouse above the waterline. It was restored in 1985 when the railings were added.

The boathouse at Kedleston Hall, designed by Robert Adam in 1770. The outer wings are wet boathouses and the centre room has a semicircular pool. Water flowing in a rill across the floor cascades through an opening into the lake. Above is a decorated fishing room, one of only three or four ever built in Britain. (Jo and Steve Turner)

Longleat, a classical boathouse on Half Mile Pond, designed by Jeffry Wyattville for the 2nd Marquess of Bath in 1807. (Jonathan Hutchins)

6

Industrial Revolution: Canal, River and Coastline – Early Modern Boathouses

'There was never from the earliest ages,' wrote Dr Johnson in 1751, 'a time in which trade so much engaged the attention of mankind, or commercial gain was sought with such genuine emulation'. The working boathouses that emerged from the late 1600s reflected the modern world. Greater political stability meant successful boat owners were better able to protect their capital assets in sturdy boathouses, allowing them to compete more effectively. Coastal landowners, freed from piracy, could safely take to their own boats, which, in the absence of roads, allowed them to visit their peers and call on their tenants. Boathouses protected their skiffs and yawls, while the structure of the boathouse provided a new opportunity for display.

Foreshore and Coastline

On the coast the earliest commercial boathouses were gig sheds. These distinctive forms emerged in the late seventeenth century and housed the pilot boats of western Cornwall and the Isles of Scilly. Pilot gigs were slender rowing boats, approximately 9 metres long with six to eight oars. They were fast. Their design determined the form of the boathouses which were long narrow buildings, approximately 10 × 3 × 2 metres high. Typically, their rubble walls were faced by mortared stone, with the entrance facing the sea. Early boathouses were thatched, their roofs lashed down with ropes against the weather. Later roofs were replaced with pantiles.

Gig sheds reflected increasing transatlantic trade and a pilot's essential skills in navigating the treacherous western approaches. Competition was fierce between pilots, the first to reach a waiting ship received a fee for safe passage and the work of unloading the cargo.

The remains of two early nineteenth-century gig sheds have been Scheduled as Ancient Monuments at Porth Askin, near the southern tip of St Agnes. Today, gig racing continues the tradition with clubs on the islands, inlets and along the south coast.

A Sailors Wedding on the Scilly Isles by James Clarke Hook, RA, with thatched gig sheds in the background. (Brighton and Hove Museums & Art Galleries)

The remains of a gig shed at St Agnes, Isles of Scilly. This was once a thatched or slated boathouse which protected a pilot gig from the heavy weather. It probably dates to the eighteenth century when there was fierce competition to pilot ships into the harbours of Cornwall and Devon. (David Lally)

Ursula's Boat House, Durghan, Cornwall, 2023. This gig house on the Helford River is where the local gig club is based.

As the economy developed, coastal towns and ports expanded. London grew exponentially as an imperial capital drawing trade from overseas and home ports. It became a gateway to the empire and during the eighteenth and nineteenth centuries the tideway above Lambeth was the home to several barge and boat makers.

Thomas Roberts, royal bargemaster, in his will of 1808 left 'leasehold bargehouses, boathouses and warehouses situated in Archbishop's Walk, together with barges, boats, and stocks of timber, to his sons ... so long as they continue to carry on business as boatbuilders'. Another royal bargemaster, James Messenger (1862–1901), set up a boatbuilding business and 'built a large boathouse close to the Anglers Arms at Teddington, where he stored the Royal Barge'. Samuel Leigh's 1829 *Panorama of the Thames from London to Richmond* illustrates Roberts and Searles' boathouses adjacent to Bishops Walk at Lambeth Palace. William Biffen established a boatbuilding business in the late eighteenth century at Hammersmith, later moving to the Anchor, today the site of the Auriol Kensington Rowing Club. Biffen later built the larger Metropolitan Boathouse on Lower Mall to concentrate on the growing enthusiasm for rowing. Boathouses belonging to lightermen were to be found at Lambeth near St Mary's new chapel and upstream as far as Kew Wharf.

At many coastal ports, goods were transhipped from centres inland for export or forwarded from overseas. Typically, boathouses in these circumstances combined warehousing with protection for the skiffs and lighters essential when transferring cargo. Few survive. One is on the Brunswick Wharf at Barnstaple on the River Taw estuary in Devon. The listed boathouse is a rectangular two-storey slatestone building with one room on each floor built by the Gould family in about 1829. The boat bay on the ground floor is protected by large wooden doors opening onto the quayside. A second warehouse at Lanteglos-by-Fowey on the Pont Pill also combines boathouse and warehousing. Built in the early nineteenth century, it was located at the head of a small, sheltered creek east of the port of Fowey in Cornwall.

The combined boathouse and warehouse at Brunswick Wharf, Barnstaple, Devon. Used to store goods transhipped from ocean-going freighter to riverboats and carts, the lighters were kept on the quayside and on the ground floor. (Alamy)

Fowey had developed as a result of mining and quarrying and by the 1800s it was prospering from pilchard fishing. Today, boathouses, fish cellars and warehouses line the quays of the estuary forming the core of the historic centres of Fowey and Polruan.

One of the most distinctive boathouses related to the fishing industry is the Coronation Boathouse at Banham Quay, Kingsbridge, on the River Avon. Built in 1937 in Tudor vernacular with a jettied, rendered first floor, it has a thatched roof. It commemorates the Coronation of King George VI and was designed by J. B. Sebastian Comper. According to the listed building description, it is part of a group of buildings of an evolved pilchard fishing community that was established in the eighteenth century, and carefully managed as part of the wider estate ever since.

Many coastal boathouses in use today originated as sail lofts, warehouses or fish cellars. Boathouses specifically intended to house fishing boats reflect the vernacular character of the coastline. On the east coast there are few boathouses other than the weatherboarded fisherman's huts, sail lofts, yacht stores, granaries and boatyards that characterise many south- and east-coast ports. In the North East, where coal was shipped southwards from Newcastle and the South Yorkshire coalfields, no significant boathouses were built until the coastguard and lifeboat stations of the late eighteenth century.

In Scotland the number of historic fishing and ferry boathouses grew in the nineteenth century. On Little Cumbrae Isle and Fairlie on the Firth of Clyde, for example, two were probably built in the late eighteenth century. Located at the corner of a small walled quay, the substantial rectangular stone building with large wooden doors and a ridged roof with a modern boathouse adjacent served the nearby castle, while another to the east housed the ferry boat for the lighthouse. Boathouses at Port an Obain on Colonsay and North Uist also probably housed fishing boats and a ferryboat, and on the east coast small boathouses at Newton Point, Littleferry and Stratsteven were home to herring boats in the late nineteenth and early twentieth centuries. At Littleferry, the tiny slate-roofed boathouse is listed.

Boathouse and warehouse combined at Polruan on the River Fowey, Cornwall. These were used for goods in transit such as wine and fish, as well as for repairing and building small boats in the nineteenth century.

A nineteenth-century fishing boathouse on Cumbrae Slip on Little Cumbrae Isle in the Firth of Clyde. The boathouse housed the ferryboat and fishing boat of the estate. In the early twentieth century, the island's owner, Evelyn Stuart Parker, created a new 'mansion house' from a single-storey farmhouse. The gardens were laid out by Gertrude Jekyll and the lighthouse repaired. (JNL Fells)

Communication between landowners was important. The suppression of the Jacobite Rebellion in the Sound of Mull by the navy in 1746 had wiped out the area's boatbuilding traditions. However, in 1793, the *Old Statistical Account* entry for Morvern recorded twelve or fourteen barges, the latter 'well-rigged, the property of the gentlemen tacksmen [tenant farmers], for transporting themselves occasionally to the neighbouring islands, and for other purposes of usefulness and convenience'. 'Barges' refers to rowing or sailing gigs, wherrys or smacks which may have been imported as kits from Norway. They were kept in boathouses on the shoreline.

'No house of any pretention [on the Sound of Mull] was without a boathouse'. As late as 1902, before the construction of roads, they were 'more necessary than a stable' as landowners travelled in their own boats. The boathouse at Drimin had a boat keeper's cottage nearby and the Macleans of Coll travelled complete with a piper, while others had their 'pipers in the bow, Tartan and ribbons fluttering in the breeze'. These were designed boathouses, not simply the vernacular. Although there was one now-lost example built of timber, the majority are snecked rubble – walls built of large stones in rough courses with gaps filled by smaller stones. Clearly, the early nineteenth-century possession of a boathouse was a sign of status.

Some early boathouses on the Sound had thatched roofs, but slate was more durable and could be brought in by sea. They were terraced into sloping ground above the high-water mark and had large wooden doors. These boathouses were all dry with shingle floors, except Torosay which was paved in brick. The most elaborate is the L-shaped Gothic Achranich boathouse, an earlier building extended in 1853. Presently, the boathouse has glazed lancet windows and an adjacent room.

Further north at the top of the Sound, fishing boats were protected by nausts, stone shelters but without roofs. The remains of another boathouse on the Isle of Ewe, constructed by John Mackenzie of the Gairloch estate in the 1850s, was the boarding point for a model farm he had established on the island.

Further north still, the parallel stone walls of the traditional naust are found on the more exposed and sparsely populated north coast. To the south along the eastern seaboard boatyards and lifeboat houses characterise the coastal ports, although there are occasionally isolated boathouses such as the rowing club at Findhorn on the Murray Firth.

Boathouses on the Welsh coast are rare. Only five were identified in a survey of 2012, one of which was the lifeboat house at Porth yr Ogof. On Bardsey Island a brick-built boathouse housed the local ferryboat which supported the lighthouse. On the Menai Straits a small group provided shelter for skiffs or rowing boats belonging to the coastal estates. One was part of a secret walled garden at Brynsiencyn. Another on the Vaynol estate to the north, built between 1840 and 1855, has a veranda, supported by columns, a recurring feature of houses on the estate. The Vaynol boathouse was directly opposite another small quay at Plas Newydd on Anglesey.

In 1705, the Isle of Man was outside the Customs Union introduced by the Act of Union 1707. Rum, tobacco and brandy from Europe were landed legally, then smuggled to customers in Ireland. The towns of Castletown, Douglas and Peel all became wealthy during this period. Between 1789 and 1793 an unusual tidal boathouse was built in the harbour mouth of Castletown by George Quayle, politician and bank owner. It housed the schooner *Peggy* and was accessible only at low tide when the boat may have been used to smuggle contraband to Ireland. When Quayle died *Peggy* was laid up in the boathouse for almost 120 years until it was rediscovered in 1935. It was the only surviving shallop on the island and, with the boathouse, became part of the Manx Nautical Museum.

The boathouse at Achranich, at the head of Loch Aline, was built in 1852–53 for Octavius Smith, but predated his new house, Ardtornish Tower (1856–59, 1864–66). (David Baird)

Canalside

Boathouses are not readily associated with canals, but a small and important group represents a short period of competition for passenger traffic between canal, stagecoach and railways. From the 1780s until the 1840s, packet boats travelling at about 10 miles an hour were faster and more comfortable than the stagecoach. They could carry up to seventy passengers with heated cabins and onboard refreshments and were maintained in special boathouses, two of which survive today – one at Lancaster, the other at Droylsden near Manchester.

The 'old boathouse' in Lancaster was built in *c.* 1820 for the Lancaster Canal Company. It was intended to house and repair the 'fast packet boats' on the 57-mile route from Kendal to Lancaster and Preston. The boathouse is built of stone, two storeys high with seven bays originally over a wet dock. The northern end of the boathouse was spayed to allow the long narrow boats access to the canal without elaborate manoeuvring. When the passenger service closed in 1846 it became a warehouse. The Lancaster boathouse has been described as unique, but a second packet boathouse was built in 1833 at Droylsden on the Manchester and Ashton-under-Lyne Canal. This is a more modest single-storey stone-built building, designed to house a boat with a 'boat hole' or entrance at one end below the date stone. Unlike the Lancaster boathouse, this one is nearly parallel to the canal.

The old boathouse on the Lancaster Canal before conversion to residential use. Originally the boathouse was used to store and maintain the packet boat, which carried passengers between Kendal, Lancaster and Preston. In 1990, when it was converted to apartments, the wet dock was filled and the historic interior lost. (Clem Rutter)

The former packet boathouse at Droylsden, Lancashire, built in 1833 on the Manchester and Ashton-under-Lyne Canal. It is not far from the Canal Agent's House. The town had cotton mills, print and dye works, and a chemical works. There was a constant stream of passengers to and from Manchester. (Doctorneroli)

One of the earliest canals was opened by the Duke of Bridgewater in 1761 to carry coal from his mines in Worsley to Manchester and from the beginning packet boats served Warrington and Manchester. By the early nineteenth century, a new boathouse had been built at Worsley possibly to house a packet boat. It is a long narrow building with a pitched roof, double gates, an elliptical brick arch below a castellated parapet; unlike the other packet boathouses, this one is perpendicular to the canal. Although initially successful, profits from the canal fell in competition with the railways, but nevertheless by 1851 the canal was owned by the Earl of Ellesmere who hosted a visit by Queen Victoria and Prince Albert. Staying at Worsley Hall, Ellesmere used his boathouse to accommodate a state barge as the royal couple were taken on the canal between Patricroft station and Worsley Hall. Apparently, the water was dyed blue.

Towards the end of the nineteenth century, several affluent owners of homes such as Elmsfield, Haverbreaks, near Lancaster, built boathouses on the canal banks.

More prosaic are the functional boathouses in which narrow boats were maintained or repaired. At Ellesmere, the early boathouse designed by Thomas Telford and William Jessop, built in about 1806, covers a dry dock and is described 'as the best-preserved canal workshop site in Britain'.

By the early twentieth century, many canals were owned by railway companies, described by George Westhall in *Inland Cruising on the rivers and canals of England and Wales* (1908) as becoming 'moribund'. Despite this recreational boating was on the increase. On the Macclesfield Canal the Great Central Railway 'encourages pleasure boating on these canals and the tolls charged are merely nominal and they are admirably adapted

The boathouse on the Bridgewater Canal at Worseley, near Manchester. This is probably a packet boathouse built in the early nineteenth century but is reputed to have been built to house a royal barge for Queen Victoria's visit in 1851.

The boathouse and dry dock at Ellesmere, Shropshire, built in 1806. To empty the dock of water a temporary dam was built across the entrance by dropping 'stop-planks' into iron-shod grooves. The water was then drained, the boat coming to rest on baulks of timber in the dry dock.

to pleasure boating'. The result was a new generation of small boathouses built along the line of the canals. Some were in the grounds of large houses, others on the opposite side to the tow path and used to store rowing boats and punts. There were larger versions for motor cruisers, but few of these survive. Even more substantial boathouses such as that built in 1906 by A. J. Harmsworth at Frimley Green on the Basingstoke Canal, where boats could be hired, have been demolished. In Leicestershire, George Saunders, interviewed by Leicester University in 1985, recalled Aylestone in the 1930s. He became owner of the boathouse on the Union Canal in 1935, creating a boat hire and repair business, only to have it requisitioned in the Second World War. One well-known survivor is the colourful Edinburgh Union Canal Society boathouse where rowing boats can be hired in the summertime.

Today the canal system has few surviving boathouses – some remain from an almost forgotten period of passenger travel. Others are a reminder that recreation has been a constant feature of the canals from the beginning, an indicator of their changing role and status.

The Ashley Terrace Boathouse, near Harrison Park in the Polwarth area of Edinburgh, is the base of the Edinburgh Union Canal Society. The iconic boathouse stores rowing boats for hire on the canal during the summer. Originally on the site of the present University Boathouse, it was dismantled in 1987 and rebuilt on its present site. (Alamy)

7

The Long Nineteenth Century: Variety, Fashion and the Unexpected

The boathouses of the nineteenth century are far from the 'relatively simple, purpose-built boathouses' of conventional interpretation. Many express the partnership between designer and landowner, changing attitudes to land use and status. Fashions were changing as emphasis shifted towards enjoyment, comfort and privacy. The clients of landscape designers Capability Brown and Humphrey Repton had been rich and landed, but by 1803 the mainly new urban classes 'had little taste, no vast acreages and were solicitous to increase their property rather than enjoy it' remarked Repton in 1816. Despite this, boathouse designs would reflect fashion as the Victorians embraced variety and the unexpected.

Private Pleasures

The end of the Napoleonic Wars and post-war agricultural recession was a time of uncertainty. At Skegby in Lincolnshire a boathouse designed as a dryad temple in 1803 was a memorial to Nelson's victory on the Nile in 1801: 'Ye Nymphs and Naiads hither join and sing, To celebrate the annals of George our king'. Yet, Skegby's design was old fashioned. Within a generation neo-Tudor was in the ascendancy, captured by T. J. Ricauti's 1842 pattern book description of 'An Idea for a Rustic Fishing Cottage'.

Most picturesque Elizabethan boathouses were simpler than Ricauti's design. Bowood, Wiltshire, for example, built after 1847, part of the Italianate garden designs by George Kennedy, is half-timbered with a flanking gallery and lake-front balcony over the boat portal. Many were simpler still. At Elvaston Castle, Derbyshire, and Dudmaston in Shropshire, the Gothic boathouses, built in the 1840s, are built of brick with no more than decorative barge boards and clay-tiled roofs.

Tudor revival designs drew directly on secular elements: hood mouldings, finials and lancet windows. The results are nevertheless entirely contemporary. At Crom Castle, County Fermanagh, the 1841 boathouse is bastion-like with a Gothic arched entrance, crenelated parapet and an ornate cottage perched on top. Sir William Pilkington's boathouse west of

The boathouse at Dudmaston Hall, Shropshire, lies on the south side of the Big Pool, with views up to the hall. The substantial Broseley brick boathouse of around 1865 has two Gothic-arched entrances to the water. (Alamy)

Crom Castle, County Fermanagh, was built in 1840, designed by the English architect Edward Blore. The boathouse on the shore of Lough Erne, was rebuilt by George Sudden in 1841 in a Tudor style. It has arched doors and windows at ground-floor level. Upstairs is a room which overlooks the lake. (Andreas F. Borchert)

Tortworth Court, Gloucestershire, now a hotel, was built between 1849 and 1853. The boathouse at the north end of the lake is part of a surprise view of the house when approaching from the south. It was built in Tudor style, designed in 1850 by the architect S. S. Teulon. (Alamy)

Chevet Hall, near Wakefield (now Newmiller Dam), similarly combines a crenelated façade with hood mouldings topped by a single-storey cottage.

In contrast, several thatched and wooden-framed boathouses, such as those on the South Walsham estate or on the Edwardian How Hill estate, both in Norfolk, reflect the romanticism associated with the local vernacular. Others such as that at Warwick Castle, which housed an electric boat for the earl in 1895, combine elaborate Tudor timberwork with the primitivism of a thatched roof.

The Tudor boathouse was a popular addition to existing landscape parks. Many were situated for convenience and practicality, where possible combining variety with surprise. At Bowood the boathouse is approached through a wooded headland and appears unexpectedly east of the main house.

The role of the boathouse in entertaining visitors increased as Britain emerged from recession and the grand tour experience in Italy stimulated a new wave of Italianate gardens. Especially influential was the remodelled Capability Brown landscape at Trentham, Staffordshire, where Charles Barry, architect of the Houses of Parliament, created a garden in the 1830s. It included a low-vaulted boathouse beneath balustrading and a terrace at the north end of the lake. Although it played only a minor visual role in the intricate aesthetic of the garden, it stored the gondolas on which a gondolier in costume would ferry guests to the islands on the lake.

Trentham was pure theatre. It followed a pattern set by earlier Chinese and Oriental gardens in the 1820s when landowners sought to recreate landscapes they had seen while touring or working overseas. The fanciful nature of these early buildings can be judged from William Daniell's 1829 landscape of boathouse, fishing temple and tents at Virginia Water, now in the Royal Collection.

Displays of such wealth were not restricted to boathouse design. In 1859, the Park Place boathouse on the Thames near Henley contained 'some fine, and several remarkable, works of Art, statues, pictures, woodcarvings, and foreign curiosities ...' explained Mr and Mrs Hall in *The Book of the Thames.*

The boathouse at Trentham Gardens. The Italianate garden designed by Charles Barry, which was added to the Capability Brown landscape, included this boathouse. It is part of the terracing at the end of the lake on the River Trent.

Theatre and the unexpected are evident in the creation of another unusual boathouse form, the boat cave, a combination of natural spectacle with the unexpected. The origin of the fashion lay in the eighteenth century. One of the earliest is the rock-built boathouse at Cusworth, near Doncaster, which was part of the reworking of the estate's hydrology by John Woods between 1761 and 1765. Famous for his work at Bath and his interest in Stonehenge, Woods designed the low, vaulted faux cavern intended to house boats from which visitors emerged unexpectedly into an unknown landscape. There is a similar cavern at Stourhead.

The large stones used to form the caves were expensive and towards the end of the nineteenth century, pulhamite, a fabricated stone, was a cheaper and more flexible alternative. A boat cave for Prince Edward, the future Edward VII, at Sandringham, part of a contract to construct 'Waterfalls, rocky stream, and cave for boathouse' in 1868, signalled royal approval.

Novelty was a characteristic of the period. At Dumbleton, Gloucestershire, a boat cave was built on a small pond of just over an acre, while at Aldenham, Hertfordshire, another boat cave may have been built by the inventor James Pulham for Vicary Gibbs, barrister, gardener and plant collector. At Gunnersbury Park Lionel de Rothschild rejected a conventional design in favour of converting a former tile kiln into a Gothic-styled boathouse. Pulhamite was used to secure the footings and repair the stonework on the shoreline of the Potomac Lake. In 1874, the conversion was an exceptional commission, Rothschild reputedly investing Gunnersbury 'with such splendours as were unknown in England outside Her Majesty's own grounds'. More recently, Clare Sherrif, author of *Boathouses*, described the Arts and Crafts boathouse at Nuneham Courtney on the Thames as 'gingerbread', though perhaps the most extraordinary is O'Hagan's boathouse, a three-storey Swiss chalet on the Thames, where Edward VII lost the freehold during a game of roulette. The boathouse was imported as a kit to go in the grounds of Riverholme, a villa built in 1882, and survives today as Hucks Boatyard at Hampton.

Valued Landscapes

Increasing affluence, rising urban populations and expanding towns were conditions which favoured investment in new, often substantial houses in waterside locations. Boathouses were luxuries which spoke of their owner's status and wealth. In many of the new locations their novel architecture and acknowledged charm contributed to a sense of place, which has shaped British national identity and where boathouses have played an important but largely unacknowledged role.

Inlets, Creeks and Foreshore

There are few locations on the British coast which combine a sheltered anchorage, shelving beaches and shallow valley sides suitable for houses and boathouses. The most familiar inlets are on the south coast such as Carrick Roads, east of Falmouth, where there are several contemporary houses and their boathouses. Lower Greatwood, for example, is a nineteenth-century boathouse, originally part of the Greatwood House estate and built in 1840. Now converted into a modern home, it was from here that the MV *Darlwyne* was lost in 1966 with thirty-one on board during a trip to Fowey. In contrast, further east along the Mylor coast is a late twentieth-century house and boathouse at Beach Cottage, Restronguet Point. Designed by John Crowther and Associates, it was glowingly described by the *Architects Journal* as 'a neat, nautical little building which from the great arc of water below shows how well the clean geometric forms of the modern movement can be set off against masses of lush vegetation'.

One of the best-known inlets is the Helford River, the setting for Daphne du Maurier's novel *Frenchman's Creek.* Boathouses are part of a landscape which has developed from the eighteenth century when the gentry enjoyed bathing and boating. Flanking the river are ornamental parkland landscapes in shallow valleys running down to the sea with boathouses at Trebah, Glendurghan, Bosahan, Trelawarren and Pedn Billy. The gardens at Trebah House were planted in the 1850s and a granite boathouse added parallel to the beach, while another at Pedn Billy was thatched with a timber frame. Some were added to smaller gardens, such as that at Bar House, adjacent to Helford Passage, or across the river at Helford. Bar House was built in the early twentieth century and the elegant stone-built, apsidal boathouse at the top of a concrete slipway housed a small yacht or skiff, a roof terrace providing views towards Penarvon Cove. More modest boathouses on the inlet take advantage of the narrow creek, although some, like Bosahan, are almost cut off from the tideway by the vegetation.

Bar House, Helford River, Cornwall. The is a 'skillet' building – a drystone technique using interleaved flat stones.

The recreated boathouse in Trebah, Cornwall. The boathouse, now a café, was made of granite from a nineteenth-century boathouse, recovered from beneath the Second World War road built to provide access to the quayside.

The Thames and Other Rivers

There were significant nineteenth-century private boathouses on many English rivers. Many are associated with riverside estates on the Welland, the Trent or Lune, such as the neo-Gothic boathouse at Halton-on-Lune in Lancashire and the Kings Mills boathouse on the Trent, part of the Donnington Park estate. At Eaton Hall Park in Cheshire, the lodge house and boathouse on the River Dee, built in 1894 for the Duke of Westminster, were part of the 'richest collection of gate lodges in Britain ... when drives and lodges were an art form in their own right' according to Mowl and Earnshaw. It is the Thames, however, with over sixty boathouses between Oxford and Richmond that is the most significant landscape.

In 1803, the 2nd Duke of Northumberland had a boathouse built for his wife at Syon House on the north bank at Richmond. Designed by Robert Mylne, it was a striking gateway to the parkland for visitors who arrived by boat. Set back from the river today, it was built when suburban development was beginning to spread upriver. Above Richmond, boathouses on estates such as Howbury Park in Crowmarsh Gifford, Park Place near Henley and Cliveden at Cookham are located among later Tudorbethan and more suburban designs. At Park Place, the boathouse, built in the 1830s, was approached from the house down Happy Valley under a bridge that was described by the antiquarian Horace Walpole in 1767 as 'composed of loose rocks that appear to have been tumbled together there, the very wreck of a deluge'. The rustic boathouse was commissioned by E. Fuller Maitland,

Howbury Park boathouse in Crowmarsh Gifford is now part of a business park. It was probably built in a Tudor style by the second owner of the Howbury Hall, Henry Williams Wynn, after 1867.

The Park Place boathouse is one of the best-known private boathouses on the Thames. It was built in the 1830s and was part of a fantasy garden landscape.

The boathouse at Cliveden was designed by G. Devey and built in 1860 for the Duchess of Sutherland. The duchess had bought the estate as a retreat from London, close to her friend Queen Victoria at Windsor. (Colin Smith)

Waterside Villas, Burcot, near Oxford. The Edwardian boathouse is now a home in the grounds of the former Leonard Cheshire Home.

The Velma boathouse, Hampton Wick, in 1895 when the River Thames froze. It was designed by the architect Roland Plumbe for Dr John Langton Down and may have been intended as a memorial to his son who had died in 1883, shortly before it was built.

MP for Wallingford, who bought Park Place in 1824. The original had statues of saints in niches. Maitland, who voted against the Catholic Relief Act of 1929, may have intended them as an endorsement of the new high church ritualism that lay behind his failure to be elected at Abingdon in 1830. Although sailing and rowing were growing in popularity, in 1857 the Thames was described as 'the largest navigable sewer in the world' and it was only after the River Pollution Prevention Act 1876, which made discharging raw sewage an offence, that many riverside homeowners were prepared to invest in their own private boathouses. One of the most distinctive Thames boathouses is the Velma boathouse at Hampton Wick, described in the Introduction, which was built in 1884 and once belonged to Dr John Langton Down.

The majority of later nineteenth-century boathouses were built to accommodate rowing boats, skiffs or punts, many at right angles to the bank. Very occasionally larger ones had a central flue and chimney to take a steam launch. Typically, boathouses of this period had an upstairs saloon, balcony and rear stairs. In some cases, such as the boathouse at Shillingford, the boat bay had slatted sides. It not only allowed floodwater to flow through but provided an area where the men could change into swimming clothes, their modesty intact. Few are represented in art. *Water Willow*, a portrait of William Morris's wife, Jany Burden, by the Pre-Raphaelite painter Gabriel Rossetti in 1871, is one of the few paintings with a landscape background that includes both Kelmscott and the boathouse on the Thames. Together they situate their affair at Kelmscott which was carried on with the knowledge of Morris, a leading light in the Arts and Crafts movement.

English Lakes

In the nineteenth century, the Lake District was a magnet for the newly rich. Among the earliest was Thomas English, described as a founder of St Pancras Hospital and who built the fantasy landscape 'Belle Isle' on Windermere's largest island. The long stone-built boathouse, designed by John Plaw, had a lake-facing boat portal and a landward entrance beneath a blind Venetian window. It was not well received. Contemporaries resented the intrusion of house and boathouse. Dorothy Wordsworth, wife of the Lakeland poet, thought that 'one of the pleasantest spots on earth had been deformed by man'.

Another industrialist, Joseph Pocklington, son of a Newark banker, built Derwent Isle in the 1780s, a fantastic landscape peppered with sham buildings such as the Druid temple and stone circle. Pocklington was described by William Wordsworth as playing 'strange pranks by his buildings and plantations upon Vicar's Island'. His boathouse, in Gothic style with lancet windows and a small bell tower with a cross on top, was nonetheless a practical building, allowing him to indulge in mock naval battles and regattas. Out of sight of the house, it was not intended to catch the eye.

In contrast, the large boathouse at Wray Castle, on Windemere, designed by the Liverpool architect John Jackson Lightfoot for James Dawson, was intended to provide a spectacular foretaste of the house to come. A similar effect was created at Hallsteads on Ullswater, where the gate lodge and one of the estate boathouses were combined. Unparalleled is the boathouse row at Fell Foot on Lake Windemere. The original boathouse was probably built before 1807, near a ford across the lake, and in the 1850s, the row was extended by Colonel George Ridehalgh, director of the North Lonsdale Iron and Steel Company. Ridehalgh was a keen sailor and master of the Windermere Harriers, who used his boats to ferry his dogs around the lake. The centrepiece is a large dry boathouse intended as a talking point among his friends and yachting enthusiasts, the five boathouses including cranes and gas heating as well as storage for boats and equipment.

The Wray Castle boathouse at Low Wray Bay on Windermere was built in 1847 for the owner James Dawson (1779–1875). It was intended to impress callers and give them a foretaste of the house to come. It is now owned by the National Trust. (Ian Capper)

The row of boathouses and docks at Fell Foot on Windemere. It was built in 1869 for Colonel Ridehalgh, a keen sailor.

Norfolk and Suffolk Broads

In eastern England the rivers Bure, Yare and Ant form the framework of the Norfolk and Suffolk Broads. This 'Watery Playground' was created by peat digging, and from the eighteenth century local landowners used the rivers and broads for recreation. Towards the end of the century, 'water frolics' at Wroxham, Yarmouth and Thorpe St Andrew became important social events and many landowners owned pleasure craft which they kept in boathouses on the rivers.

In 1837, for example, the *Maria* of Yarmouth, winner of the Lowestoft Regatta, was sold to Sir Jacob Preston of Beeston Hall, who kept it in a thatched boathouse off Barton Broad. The *Maria,* sailing on the day Britain declared war on Germany in 1914, was taken back to the boathouse where it stayed until 1969 when it was moved to the Maritime Museum for East Anglia at Yarmouth.

Recreational boating on the Broads remained the preserve of wealthy landowners for much of the nineteenth century. A typical thatched and wooden-framed boathouse on the South Walsham Broad, recently restored by the Fairhaven Garden Trust, was originally part of the South Walsham estate. Later in the century, as the Broadlands became accessible by train, the Bure and Yare rivers were compared to the Thames by G. Christopher Davies, whose illustrations include the thatched boathouses near Salhouse Dyke: 'an old-world picture: a boat-builder's shed, large and old, of picturesque construction, stands on the margin, amid low bushes and under the shade of mighty trees. Beneath it is a large boat and a wherry sleepily awaiting repair ... on Hickling Broad a remarkably neat boathouse had boats for hire'.

At the northern end of Hickling Broad, part of the Hickling Broad estate, are sixteen striking boathouses and punt sheds. These late nineteenth- and early twentieth-century timber and thatched boathouses are leased to the Norfolk Wildlife Trust and figure prominently in publicity about the Broads.

Recreational use of the Broads from the early twentieth century led to an increase in the construction of boathouses, staithes and summerhouses. Many continue the rural tradition, such as the listed White Lodge boathouse, designed in 1938, where Arthur Ransome wrote *Coot Club,* the fifth book in the 'Swallows and Amazons' series. The boathouse has weatherboard walls and eyebrow thatch over the rear entrance to a wet dock with a flanking walkway which allowed passengers to step aboard the boats. During the later twentieth century, the river frontages of Wroxham, Horning and Stalham saw the creation of substantial suburban riverside houses, with many accompanied by boathouses.

Thatched boathouses on Hickling Broad, Norfolk. At the northern end of Hickling Broad, these were part of the Hickling Broad estate and were used to store punts and marshman's boats from the late nineteenth and early twentieth centuries. (Adrian S. Pye)

Reservoirs and Meres

The association between Rudyard Kipling and Rudyard Lake, after which he was named, is well known. The lake was a reservoir for the Trent and Mersey Canal and created on land belonging to the Earl of Macclesfield. Initially treated as the earl's private lake, Charles Barry, who redesigned Eynsham Hall for the 5th Earl, was probably responsible for designing an elegant sandstone boathouse in 1843–45. In 1847, the canal company was bought by the North Staffordshire Railway and by the 1890s it was aggressively promoted as a place to live. Over fourteen boathouses were built on its banks. Horton Lodge and Challenors, Brackens and Bilton are all exuberant Edwardian designs, but the most spectacular is the Lady of the Lake. Built in 1893, it was designed for the Davenport family, silk manufacturers from Leek, and recently described by the *Daily Mail* as 'picture perfect'.

Lesser known are the meres of north Shropshire – small glacial lakes, long the focus for sailing and boating. Several – such as those at Hanmer Mere, Colemere and Crose Mere – have estate boathouses, though the largest is at Ellesmere. On the east bank of the lake is the terracing of the Italianate garden at Oteley, which was completed in 1851. The garden was designed by the owner after a honeymoon tour to Italy and has terraces ranged around a central axis that descends to an elevated terrace above the twin-portalled boathouse. Comparable to Trentham, it has been described as Shropshire's most spectacular Italianate garden.

This boathouse on Rudyard Lake, Staffordshire, was probably designed by Charles Barry in 1843–45 for the Earl of Macclesfield. Barry had worked for the earl on his house at Eynsham in Oxfordshire in 1843.

The Lady of the Lake boathouse on Rudyard Lake, Staffordshire, was built in 1893. It was designed by the Leek architect William Larner Sugden for the Davenport family. (Alamy)

The twin portals of the Italianate boathouse at Oteley, Shropshire. The boathouse is near derelict, though there are plans for its restoration.

The boathouse on Hanmer Mere, Shropshire, built in the nineteenth century as part of the Hanmer estate. On the landward gable is an armorial with two lions passant and the motto 'Gaurdez L'onnheur'. Sir John Hanmer (1809–81) pulled down Hanmer Hall and the family now live in Bettisfield Hall, south-east of the mere.

Lochs and Loughs

The nineteenth century was the 'High Summer' of Scottish architecture. Although drawing on common traditions of landscape design and architectural practice with England, there were important differences.

One of the earliest boathouses was that at Pitfour, known as the 'Blenheim of the North', near Aberdeen. The boathouse, built for the 4th Laird by John Smith, was a Gothic-arched imitation 'ruin'. Later boathouses had upstairs saloons, balconies, elaborate landing stages and retiring rooms. Dochfour boathouse, built in 1864, had deep eaves and a sheltered balcony with external stairs to an upper chamber.

As the century progressed, Scottish boathouse design became increasingly extravagant. On the west coast of the Isle of Arran, the Dougarie boathouse, built in 1885 by the Glasgow architect John James Burnett for the 11th Duke of Hamilton, was used for sailing on the Kilbrannon Sound. It was also a place for entertaining guests, its twin gables,

Dougarie boathouse on the Isle of Arran was built in 1885 by the Glasgow architect John James Burnett for the 11th Duke of Hamilton. It was used for sailing on the Kilbrannon Sound and as a place for entertaining guests such as Prince Rainer and Princess Antoinette of Monaco. (Alamy)

Pitfour was improved by James Ferguson between 1777 and 1820. He was the 3rd Laird and added the lake and canal to the estate. The boathouse was built deliberately to look like a ruin. (Oliver Dixon)

widely swept eaves and long slipway providing views of the sea and the Isle of Arran. The interior was decorated with caricatures by the *Vanity Fair* artist Liberio Prosperi. At Manderston, the boathouse, built in 1894, was designed in a whimsical Swiss-chalet style by the Scottish architect John Kinross to celebrate the engagement of its owner, Sir James Miller, to Eveline Curzon, daughter of Lord Scarsdale, whose family home was Kedleston in Derbyshire. Equally whimsical at Mount Melville, now Craigtoun Park near St Andrews, the Manchester architect John Waterhouse designed a Dutch village which included a boathouse for Dr James Younger of the brewing dynasty in 1920. The most extravagant was the granite boathouse, combined with two immense four-storey portal towers, built in 1922–23 at the entrance to the Dunecht estate, near Aberdeen. It was described by Tim Buxbaum, author of *Scottish Garden Buildings*, as the 'last gasp' of the boathouse building tradition.

In the nineteenth century, Ireland was part of the United Kingdom, and the shorelines of sea and inland loughs provided sites for boathouses comparable to those on the mainland. Inland, the Tudor-style Crom Castle boathouse, on the shore of Lough Erne and designed by George Sudden in 1841, like those on the Sound of Mull, was intended to impress and welcome visitors as they stepped ashore. The same principle lay behind Dickinson boathouse on the Castle Ward estate, Downpatrick, where the Georgian house overlooks Strangford Lough. At Myra Castle, also overlooking Strangford Lough, the boathouse, built between 1840 and 1850 when the parkland was set out by Rowland Craig-Laurie, included a small quay intended to take in coal. It was, as the garden designer John Julius Loudon put it, another concession 'to the enjoyment of real life'.

Dunecht, on Loch Skene, combined a boathouse and four-storey towered gate lodges, built in 1922–23. It was described as 'the last gasp' of the Scottish boathouse building tradition. (Dreamstime)

8

The Boathouse as Clubhouse

During the sixteenth century, at ports around the country local watermen waited afloat for ships to arrive before racing to be the first alongside and win the contract to unload their cargo. Competition was fierce. In 1571, the earliest boat racing was recorded at Gravesend, and by 1661 Pepys described 'wager racing'. These were often fixed and by 1722 the gentry were organising their own races. Dry boathouses on the coast had provided the workshops and stores for working skiffs, but recreational rowing saw riverside inns provide boathouses where the publican stored, repaired and hired boats. These were the origins of a new type of boathouse with club rooms, changing rooms and lockers as well as boat bays, equipment stores and sometimes accommodation.

Rowing and Sculling

The early pubs were often close to ferry crossings and among the earliest were the boathouse inns at Preston on the River Ribble and Salford on the River Irwell. Both became centres for professional racing in the early nineteenth century. Similar arrangements emerged on the Thames, with boathouses attached to pubs such as the Red House at Battersea and the Folly Tavern at Oxford, which supplied boats to students and townspeople alike.

In the early 1800s, rowing clubs proliferated. Some were largely amateur and others were more professional, with competing clubs established to represent boat-builders, hirers and publicans. Snobbery soon infected otherwise friendly competition as attempts were made to separate the professional from the gentleman amateur. As the century progressed, professional rowers, who were often seasonally unemployed, were gradually excluded from club rowing.

In London commercial boathouses played a key role in the emergence of amateur rowing. These were typically dry, combining clubrooms, boat storage and a landing wharf. The early Thames clubs were located close to the city, but during the mid-nineteenth century rowers were forced off the water by increased traffic, bridges and pollution. By mid-century, the area near Searle's Yard at Stangate, opposite the Palace of Westminster, was one of 'dark tenements, rotten wharves, dirty boathouses'. It was the same in other cities too, such as Manchester and Newcastle. The result was a move upstream to more rural locations.

An important aspect of the early clubs was formal dining, and with the move upstream the boathouse became more elaborate. On the Thames several clubs moved to the village of Putney where a boathouse row was created. One of the earliest and most substantial was that of the London Rowing Club, built in 1871. The club had rented rooms at the Star and Garter pub from 1856, and its boats were stored at Searle's Yard, Putney. Its first boathouse was built in 1857 on Finches Field. It was a 'sort of a box', 70 × 39 feet and made of wood with a felt roof, three doors to boat bays, a side door and barred window at each end. This was not an immediate success. It leaked, and by 1868 there were complaints that it was too small. In 1869, the club was incorporated as a limited company with capital of £2,000 for a new boathouse. Designed by the architect and club secretary George Dunnage, it was 'the most momentous development' in the life of the club and was working by March 1872. Dunnage represented the social character of the club and was well placed to promote the new design. It provided boat bays below a large clubroom, with lockers for rent and a grandstand on the third floor to accommodate spectators at the Oxford and Cambridge university boat race. As the club grew, it was extended in 1905 by four bays to its present size.

The London club had a large membership drawn from smaller clubs facing closure, but not all joined in. The Leander club, with only twenty-five members, moved from Searle's Yard in 1860 and built their boathouse adjacent to the London in 1867. Also two storeys, their balcony area was supported on cast-iron columns, which projected over the brick-built boat bays. Leander was to grow in size and status, building the Pink Palace at Henley in 1897.

The London Rowing Club boathouse at Putney was established in this rural village when rowing clubs moved out of central London. The club was first based at the Star and Garter pub, then moving to a shed-like boathouse before the present one was built in 1871.

Some clubs located even further upriver. In a pioneering move, Frederick J. Furnival, co-founder of the National Amateur Rowing Association in 1890, intended to counter the 'snobbish and exclusive definition of the term amateur' and launched the Hammersmith Sculling Club for Girls in 1896. With premises on Lower Mall, Hammersmith, the club was soon known as the Furnivall Sculling Club.

By 1898 there were some 457 rowing clubs in Britain, many on inland waters and many upstream from the earlier estuary or dockside sites. Boathouses were often constructed with the help of rich sponsors. In the North West the elegant half-timbered Grosvenor Rowing Club boathouse at Chester, designed by T. M. Lockwood in 1877, was supported by the 1st Duke of Westminster. The club was founded in 1869 to serve 'the clerks and assistants in the city'. In Shrewsbury a brick-built boathouse with club rooms above the boat bays, designed by the architect J. Randall in 1881 for the Pengwern Boat Club, has an impressive presence on the river.

The Furnivall Sculling Club was founded in 1896 as the Hammersmith Sculling Club for Girls. The club bought the premises at Nos 19 and 20a Lower Mall for £750 in 1912. It had previously been a coffee house and while the cottage at No. 20a housed a resident housekeeper, boat racks were needed in No. 19. (Alamy)

The Grosvenor Rowing Club, Chester, was founded to provide recreation for the less-fortunate sportsmen in Chester. It was built in 1877 and supported by the Duke of Westminster.

Pengwern Boathouse, Shrewsbury, was built on a site bought in 1880. Constructed in 1881, it comprises a three-storey, half-timbered clubhouse above boat bays. It has been compared to the former Oxford University Boat Club, destroyed by fire in 1999.

Modern and eighteenth-century boathouses at Eton on the River Thames. Although belonging to Eton School, the central building (with the hipped roof) was let out to 'The Brocas Boat House Limited, Boats to let' in the 1870s.

In the 1780s, boys at Eton and Westminster schools had become accustomed to hiring boats from commercial boatmen, such as Tolladays. It was dangerous, but racing for wagers was common. Solid brick boathouses from the 1700s can still be seen on the north bank of the Thames from Windsor Bridge at Eton. Other schools followed suit. Rowing was established at Shrewsbury in 1839 with its boathouse at Horwoods Ferry. Durham School rowed competitively as early as 1834, but did not build its boathouse until 1892. Early school boathouses were generally boatsheds with no requirement for club facilities. Bedford School began rowing in 1861 and in 1899 the Arts and Crafts architect C. E. Mallows designed a neo-classical boathouse with clubhouse above colonnaded boat bays, although it was too expensive and never built.

School rowing developed throughout the century, but it was the universities which gained the limelight. The first Oxford and Cambridge boat race took place in 1829 and while Oxford relied on barges, by the 1840s they were becoming impractical. In 1880, a boathouse was designed for the university by John Oldrid Scott, son of architect Sir George Gilbert Scott. The controversial boathouse was initially described as 'hideous, a monstrosity' before the design was amended and a large, imposing boathouse was built in Tudorbethan style on the Berkshire bank of the Thames.

Oxford University College Boat Club, built in 1880. The boathouse was burnt down in 1999 and replaced with an award-winning new design in the same location.

Cambridge, in contrast, adopted more restrained architecture, and by the end of the century several college boathouses had been built on the River Cam. The earliest and most striking is the Goldie Boathouse, home of the Cambridge University Boat Club, built in 1882 and named after the club president the Revd John Dashwood Goldie. Others, such as Trinity Hall boathouse, an attractive late Arts and Crafts building constructed in 1905, illustrate the changing architectural fashions of the Edwardian era.

Women had rowed competitively since the end of the eighteenth century and numbers had increased by the early twentieth century, but the sport was dominated by men. The London Rowing Club, for example, was founded for the 'encouragement of rowing on the River Thames among gentlemen amateurs'. During the struggle for women's emancipation, not only were boathouses associated with the male establishment, but they were often isolated, distant from towns or villages. Several were set alight during the campaign for women's suffrage. Rough's boathouse at Oxford was burnt down in 1913, and it has been estimated that five out of thirty-four boathouses and sports pavilions countrywide were torched in 1913.

Boathouses and clubs continued to be a challenging environment for women rowers. In 1905, Bradford on Avon Rowing Club recorded a plea from a member that 'there have been rumours and going on lately that my daughter (who is now completely ruined) first met her downfall by being enticed to the boathouse ... the boathouse has previously been used for immoral purposes ... please make it impossible for it to be used so again'. On the

The Goldie boathouse, Cambridge, home to the Cambridge University Boat Club and named after Revd John Dashwood Goldie. It was built in 1905. Women had no access to its training facilities until a small extension of changing rooms, an office and kitchen was built in 2012.

Emmanuel College boathouse, built in 1896, was extended in 1936 and again in 1993. The latest extension, designed by Thurlow Carnell and Thornburrow, almost tripled the size of the building. Today, the boathouse is home to the boat clubs of a few Cambridge University colleges, Emmanuel, Hughes Hall, Lucy Cavendish, and that of Anglia Ruskin University.

Dart, although women were able to join the Dartmouth Rowing Club in 1936, they were not allowed in the boathouse and the men carried their boat to the water. Such prejudice lasted well into the late twentieth century.

Rowing largely ceased during the First World War. Worthing Amateur Boat Club shut its boathouse, sold the furniture and the boats were stowed away until it reopened in 1920. The average mortality rate for rowing club members approached one-third. Didsbury Rowing Club, formed in a suburb of Manchester in 1850, opened a new half-timbered boathouse in 1909 to accommodate over 100 members. It closed when it was evident that all the members of the club had been killed during the war.

Membership numbers improved after the war and some successful clubs were able to build new boathouses. In 1921, Bedford Modern School raised the money to build a three-sectioned boathouse. A traditional design by the local architect John Allen, it is shared with Bedford Modern School Boat Club and Bedford Girls' School Rowing Club. The boys at Radley, Oxfordshire, built their own shed-like boathouse in 1921, organised by the Revd Vyvyan Hope. But the depression of the 1930s saw many clubs fail or amalgamate for survival.

Bedford Modern School boathouse, originally Bedford Schools and Bedford Rowing Club boathouses. They were built in 1921 to a design by the architect G. R. Allen.

One of the most striking developments was on Boathouse Island at Oxford. By the 1930s the college barges moored along Christ Church Meadows, where crews changed and spectators stood on the upper decks, were beginning to disintegrate. Christ Church College, which owned the Meadows, devised a scheme for a row of boathouses between the River Cherwell and the New Cut, and by 1939 three boathouses accommodating four clubs had been built.

However, as Diana Rowntree, architecture critic of *The Guardian*, wrote: 'their effect on the landscape was one of desolation. They give the impression that everyone has gone home and left no address'. These boathouses are rare art deco brick structures designed by the Oxford practice of Bridgewater and Shepheard and were the first in a row of ten boathouses that characterise the river today. A similar art deco boathouse built by Nottingham University on the River Trent, adjacent to three nineteenth-century boathouses, was built without comment, though the extra boathouse at Trent Bridge did not quite achieve the effect of a row.

Boathouse Island, Oxford. These art deco-style boathouses – from the right, Christ Church, Magdalen College, Merton and Worcester colleges – were criticised as giving 'the impression that everyone has gone home and left no address'.

The Second World War brought further challenges. Women members of the Furnivall Sculling Club had helped it survive the First World War, but in 1940 their boathouse at No. 19 Lower Mall in London was bombed. During the war clubs suffered as members left to fight, and after 1945 many clubs combined resources. Clubs needed to diversify to survive and the boathouse was a key resource. Nigel Wigglesworth, author of the *Social History of English Rowing,* described how the Upper Thames Rowing Club, established in 1963, specifically set out to cater for the international demand for boathouse facilities by visiting clubs on the Henley stretch of the Thames. Many clubs let out their club rooms for social events as a matter of course.

Unfortunately, post-war vandalism took its toll on often isolated boathouses. At Wigan, vandalism reduced the boathouse to such a degree that it was demolished. At Bradford and Lancaster, new premises were paid for by insurance following vandalism. Despite the damage, the renewed boathouses reflected the recovering popularity of competitive and recreational rowing. In 1948, Britain hosted the Olympics with rowing at Henley, and while war and depression had left just 100 clubs, by 1950 new boathouses were beginning to appear.

At Kingston upon Thames the concrete-framed boathouse, designed by J. H. Lomas in 1970 at Canbury Gardens for the Kingston Rowing Club and Tiffin Boys School, was described as one of the best new buildings on the river. Boathouses now not only reflected the modernist architecture of the 1960s, but schools and rowing clubs were attracting more overtly avant-garde designs.

At Carmel College, the Julius Gottlieb Gallery and Boathouse, designed in 1968 by the practice of Sir Basil Spence, Bonnington and Collins, combined boathouse and gallery in a unique reinforced-concrete pyramid. It was 12.2 metres square and rose to a height of 14 metres. The 'proto-post-modern' boathouse has been described as 'the most dramatic example of the tough, geometrical forms increasingly preferred by Sir Basil Spence'.

The Julius Gottlieb Gallery and Boathouse, Carmel College. It was given to the college by Lieutenant Commander E. J. Gottlieb, a school governor, as a memorial to his father Julius Gottlieb, a designer in wood and patron of the arts.

9

Parkland to Public Parks: Leisure and Recreation in the Nineteenth and Twentieth Centuries

In 1829, John Loudon's *Breathing Places for the Metropolis* signalled the start of a campaign to develop public parks. The Select Committee on the Health of the Towns (1840) argued that improvements were essential, not only for 'the welfare of the poor' but for 'the safety of property and the security of the rich'. It was a time when radical voices understood public open spaces, and parks were expected to offer some relief to overcrowding, poverty and lack of morals.

From Parkland to Public Park

The first free-to-enter public park was Princes Park in Liverpool, designed by Joseph Paxton, head gardener at Chatsworth, Derbyshire, in 1842. It was Paxton's first independent work on an urban park and was influenced by the Chatsworth estate and Regents Park in London. The park's Swiss-chalet boathouse was probably designed by John Robertson, who until 1840 had been Loudon's principal draughtsman. Paxton went on to design the later park in Birkenhead in 1844, although his close relationship to the Duke of Devonshire meant that during construction he was preoccupied with the duke's illness. Consequently, the boathouse of 1846, commonly illustrated as the first urban boathouse, was designed by local architect Lewis Hornblower. The boathouse was inspired by Roman practice, with a vaulted boat bay beneath a tiled pavilion intended as a bandstand. In contrast, Hornblower's boathouse in Sefton Park, Liverpool, (1872) was a mock-Tudor design that followed contemporary fashion, as did the Gothic boathouse in Stanley Park (1870) by E. R. Robson.

The close relationship between private parkland boathouses and public parks was maintained into the twentieth century through the purchase of private parklands by local authorities. In many, where existing boathouses were retained, they remained entirely ornamental. At Russell Gardens, Dover, the boathouse is an Arts and Crafts eye-catcher

The 'Roman' boathouse in Birkenhead Park. In 2011, the park received a restoration grant of over £11 million from the Heritage Lottery Fund, Merseyside Objective One Programme, the European Union and Wirral Borough Council. It was the start of a major restoration project to bring the park's key treasures including the boathouse back to life. (Phil Nash)

with a tiled summerhouse and white-painted pillars over a simple brick arched boat bay. It was designed in 1899 by Thomas Mawson, the landscape designer, for the Kearsey Court garden of Alfred Leney, brewer and drinks manufacturer. The garden was acquired by Dover Council and opened as a park in 1951. At Wollaton Park, the 825-acre estate was sold to the Corporation of Nottingham in 1924–25 and opened to the public in the 1950s. The boathouse, a sham bridge at the west end of the lake built in 1774–85, remains an evocative reminder of the eighteenth-century parkland, while at North Lodge, originally Elmfield House in Darlington, the crenelated Gothic Revival boathouse (1870) is firmly in the tradition of Wray Castle or Fell Foot. Gunnersbury Park, bought from the Rothschilds, was opened to the public in 1926 and its converted but ornamental Gothic boathouse remains beside the Potomac Lake.

From the start boathouses were an important safety valve, with boating promoted as a family activity. In Hanley Park, Stoke-on-Trent, where the park and boating lake opened in 1894, it was first proposed in 1857 in a large area of wasteground called 'Stoke Fields', divided by the Cauldon Canal. The designer was Thomas Mowson and the boathouse, which continued the tradition of Tudor-inspired design, was described by Travis Elborough, the park historian, as 'Arts and Crafty', marking the point at which the Tudor style was evolving into the Edwardian leitmotif 'Tudorbethan'. Later, at Heaton Park in Manchester, bought by the city in 1902, a boating lake was created on the south side between 1908 and 1912 on the site of the Earl of Wilton's racecourse. A boathouse, built in 1923–24, represented the new cottage style of the Garden City movement and stored boats for hire.

The Heaton Park boathouse was part of a trend to design specifically for rowing boat hire in the late nineteenth century. At Pittville Park, Cheltenham, the borough surveyor Joseph Hall built the boathouse in 1894 for £90, and bought ten rowing boats to go with it. Alexandra Park, Oldham (1903), and Wardown Park, Luton (1907), both acquired elegant Edwardian boathouses with boats for hire. In central London, both Hyde Park and Regents Park received boathouses in the early twentieth century. Boating had been allowed on the Serpentine in Hyde Park since 1847 and winter skating long before, but accidents were

In Alexandra Park, Oldham, the half-timbered boathouse dominates the northern edge of the boating lake, which was created in 1903. (David Dixon)

In 1894, at Pittville Park, Cheltenham, a boathouse designed by the Borough Surveyor Joseph Hall was built for £90 on the north bank of the lake with ten boats for hire. The boathouse has not changed since it was built.

common. The Royal Humane Society, set up to treat victims in 1774, was at first based in a small cottage, but in 1902 built its own boathouse. Later, another was built to store rowing boats and was rebuilt in 1954 following wartime damage. Today both store racing shells. In the early twenty-first century, a third commercial shed-like boathouse was built by Bluebird Boats to provide rowing boats and pedaloes for hire. In Victoria Park, Northampton, and Wicksteed Park, Kettering, corrugated iron was used as an economical way of providing boat storage and repair facilities. Nor did all the pre-existing boathouses remain as antique ornaments. At Shibden, near Halifax, the hall and park were bought in 1923 by a local councillor who presented them to East Halifax District. Opened by the Prince of Wales in 1926, the former estate stone boathouse, built in 1836, stored rowing boats for hire.

Healthy living was the underlying principle behind the public park. In the early twentieth century, the concept was taken up at the first holiday resort, Thorpeness on the Suffolk coast. It was the inspiration of Glencairn Ogilvie, owner of the Sizewell estate. The idea of a holiday village was new, and it was built before the appearance of holiday camps. Ogilvie and his friends, architects W. G. Wilson (1856–1943) and Forbes Glennie

(1872–1950), created the village between 1910 and the 1920s. At its heart was a 64-acre boating lake or mere. This was an important adventure area for children, inspired by *Peter Pan* (1904), written by Ogilvie's friend J. M. Barrie, and the boathouse was one of the first buildings to be completed.

The nineteenth century was the heyday of public park boathouses as they developed from the architectural traditions of the country estate into fashionable Edwardian buildings of the early twentieth century. War took its toll as parks were requisitioned and buildings reused as stores and workshops or simply closed in the 1940s. Despite an upsurge of enthusiasm for public open space in the 1950s, the late twentieth century was to be marked by neglect, loss and vandalism.

The lake, which dominates the southern part of Heaton Park, Manchester, was created on the site of a racecourse in 1912–13. The boathouses were built at the same time as the lake on the western shore. (Ian Greig)

One of two boathouses in Hyde Park. This was built in 1902 by The Royal Humane Society to house boats in case of accidents on the Serpentine.

10

The World's Stage

At the start of the twenty-first century boathouses have been transformed. Some historic buildings have been listed for their heritage value. Several have received prestigious architectural awards; others have exceptional value in helping overcome prejudice. When Jane Kingsley, author of *Cambridge University Women's Boat Club*, was interviewed by the BBC in 2015, she attributed the team's success to their having their own boathouse. In the twenty-first century, the current generation of boathouses includes iconic buildings recognisable on the world's stage.

Modern Times

Boathouses in the mid-twentieth century were at best a minor building type. Few private boathouses were built in the 1920s and 1930s. Architecturally art deco had not produced designs which were out of the ordinary. During the Second World War many boathouses were reused, damaged or destroyed. On the Helford River, Cornwall, the Special Operations Executive (SOE) requisitioned Pedn Billy boathouse as a base from which to send agents to occupied France. In 1944, the granite boathouse at Trebah, also on the Helford River, was dynamited and the stone used in the foundation of a road and jetty where heavy equipment was loaded for D-Day, though surprisingly the granite was rediscovered in the 1960s and used to build a new boathouse.

In 1948, the revivalist spirit was maintained by the architect Francis York with a classically inspired lakeside boathouse at South Crest, Redditch, Worcestershire, and there is another by Raymond Erith, architect to No. 10 Downing Street, on the River Stour in Suffolk built for his Aunt Maud.

In the twenty-first century, some modern boathouses have proved more controversial. On the Thames at Shiplake, Kevin McCloud, the presenter of the TV series *Grand Designs*, was at the centre of a row when promoting the construction of a new boathouse, described by the programme's publicity as 'uncompromisingly modern', its design contrasting sharply with nearby Edwardian boathouses.

Above left: Raymond Erith's revivalist-style boathouse on the River Stour in Suffolk. The boathouse was inspired by the Temple of Artemis on the banks of the River Ilissus, which runs just outside the walls of Athens. It was built for the architect's Aunt Maud. (Alamy)

Above right: The 'challenging' boathouse at Shiplake on the Thames in South Oxfordshire. The boathouse was designed by architect Chris Tapp and featured in the television programme *Grand Designs*. (Alamy)

At Hampton Wick, the Velma boathouse on the Thames was mired in controversy when developers proposed to move it some 50 metres from the river and replace it with a five-storey, yacht-inspired, modernist boathouse. Ballyhoo, designed by Adrian James of Oxford, built on the Thames at Caversham and described as 'an assertive new house ... which has caused a few ripples', was advertised in 2015 as one of the most expensive homes in Berkshire.

In the 1990s, several boathouses were destroyed by fire. Arson may have destroyed the Oxford University boathouse in September 1999, while Hertford College boathouse was torched by the Animal Liberation Front protesting at the building of the South Parks Laboratory, Oxford, in 2005. In the north the Tudor revivalist boathouse in Sefton Park, Liverpool, was destroyed by arson in 2002. The Swiss Chalet boathouse in Princes Park, also in Liverpool, neglected during the 1980s, was partially destroyed by fire in the early 1990s and despite its listing status another decade of neglect resulted in its complete destruction. As the report 'Uncertain Prospects' put it, the boathouse became a symbol of corporate neglect.

Accidents took their toll. Fire was responsible for damage to the thatched boathouse at Warwick Castle when sparks from a trebuchet, a one-armed medieval catapult, spectacularly set the roof alight during a medieval fair in 2015. The Warwick boathouse has been restored, but fire at Wicksteed in Kettering led to the demolition of the functional

The new boathouse at King's School Worcester has a cantilevered prow which serves as a landmark on the embankment of the River Severn. Described by the architect John Christophers as 'a jewel-like modern incident along the embankment', the curve of the building reflects the site boundary which was the line of Worcester's Bronze Age fortification. (Alamy)

corrugated-iron boathouses that served the park's rowing boats. Built during the First World War by Charles Wicksteed, they had been part of a model village proposed for the industrial town.

Many boathouses have been repurposed with some converted to holiday lets while others are cafés, restaurants or storerooms. In Oxford, the Cherwell boathouse, built in 1904, is a restaurant where punts are still for hire. At the World Heritage Site of Saltaire, Yorkshire, the boathouse was part of the mill complex commissioned by the owner Sir Titus Salt for his workforce. It was built in 1871, when the River Aire was widened for boating and swimming. Twice damaged by arsonists, it was refurbished in 2016 and is now open as a pub. Several boathouses have musical associations. T'Pau singer Carol Decker worked as a bartender and lived at the Pengwern Boat Club in Shrewsbury for four years while writing her biggest hits. In Pangbourne at a boathouse on the Thames, John Paul Jones and John Bonham formed Led Zepplin, although today the boat bay has been converted into a heated swimming pool.

Revival and Renewal

Despite the vandalism, deliberate demolition and accidents, a new wave of purpose-built boathouses have been tagged by the architectural press as the 'new museums' – noteworthy as modernist buildings of international repute. These include the boat-shaped Kings School boathouse at Worcester and the Eton boathouse at Dorney Lake. The latter, designed by the school's architects H. J. Stribling & Partners, was built in 2006 and hosted the 2012 Olympics. In Oxford the new Oxford University College boathouse, designed by Shahriar Nassar of Belsize Architects, was awarded the prestigious Royal Institute of British Architects (RIBA) South Award in 2008. A glass and steel structure, 'the long copper roof suggests the keel of an upturned boat, and cuts through the sky like an oar through water'.

A second modern boathouse at Wallingford, by the Oxford architects Tuke Manton for Oxford University Boat Club in 2009, was also intended to complement its riverside setting. The design represents modern university rowing, with a dry boathouse for storage and maintenance of racing shells and oars and a wet boathouse for coaching launches.

Oxford University College boathouse, designed by Belsize Architects, was awarded a Royal Institute of British Architects (RIBA) prize. It was described in the press as not just a boathouse, but 'a grandstand of the first order' representing a new age in rowing. (Alamy)

Eton Rowing Centre or Boathouse at Dorney Lake was built in 2006 and is the largest boathouse in Britain. It was the centre for rowing in the 2012 Olympics. (Alamy)

Oxford University Boat Club, built in 2009 at Wallingford, was designed by Tuke Manton architects. The new boathouse has extensive facilities shared by rowers and staff alike.

New boathouses for Oxford Brookes University, south of Wallingford, were completed in 2010 in time for the 2012 Olympics. They were designed to be 'practical, a contemporary interpretation of local agricultural buildings ... clad in matt-black stained English larch to produce a subtle silhouette within the landscape', as Spratley Studios director Jeremy Spratley put it. 'The new boathouse is not glamorous or egocentric, needlessly addressing the river in some overtly arrogant manner, but is simple, clean and efficient, like its contents.'

Oxford University's more traditional rival, Cambridge, has also invested in state-of-the-art boathouses. At Ely in 2016, the boathouse, designed by Jerry Bailey, is parallel to the river. Here the setting was an important factor and a twist in the roof oriented towards the west, provided views of Ely Cathedral from the Club Room. A proposal in 2024 by Newnham College represented not only the rise in women's rowing but a sustainable turn in boathouse design. The plan is for the boathouse to have a low-carbon impact with a light footprint, a traditional form with locally felled larch, timber-framed and pitched roof. The walls will be made of woven willow and the designer intends the willow to sprout, the shoots encouraged to grow so they can be re-woven through the panels as a living willow screen.

On the coast the RNLI has adopted a conventional approach, but one which also takes setting into account. At Lyme Regis in Dorset the new stone boathouse, constructed in 1997, although blending in with other seafront buildings, was initially subject to objections that it would impact views of the famous Cobb before the design was finalised.

The open character of boathouses is ideal for museum display. In Southwold, the former Cromer lifeboat house was brought by barge in 1997. Initial reports by Peter Hoffman in the *Eastern Daily Press* described it as 'a monument to someone's egomania'. But today the boathouse has been repurposed as the Alfred Corry Museum containing the former lifeboat and is a popular local museum. On the Isle of Tiree, the Tog Studio constructed the Noust community boathouse in one week during 2013 to house the historic boats of the Tiree Maritime Trust. On a larger scale, Boathouses 4 and 6 at Portsmouth are now museum

Cambridge University boathouse, Ely. The innovative design includes views of Ely Cathedral from the clubroom on the first floor.

spaces. But perhaps the best-known boathouse museum is at Laugharne, where according to the museum website, Dylan Thomas 'worked in the Writing Shed above the Boathouse with its remarkable and inspiring views of four estuaries'.

Today, boathouses, long overlooked as a building type, are finally emerging through conservation, re-use and new design, not only reflecting the complexity and diversity of modern society, but as distinctive buildings in their own right.

Gloucester Rowing Club boathouse under construction on the banks of the Gloucester and Sharpness Canal in 2019. It is one of a new range of modern designs intended to provide facilities for several rowing clubs.

The modern boathouse on the Aylesbury Branch of the Grand Union Canal. It was completed in 2013 and is run by the Aylesbury Canal Society. Canal boats can be repaired here.

Bibliography and Further Reading

This is a short reading list, in addition to the works cited in the text, for those seeking to learn more about boathouses and some of the people and organisations associated with them.

Buxbaum, Tim, *Scottish Garden Buildings: From Food to Folly* (Edinburgh: Mainstream 1989)

Ebsworth, Julian, *On Finches Field The Home of London Rowing Club Since 1871* (London: London Rowing Club, 2023)

Martin, Colin J. M., and Martin, Paula F. De C., 'Marine Boathouses of the Sound of Mull', *International Journal of Nautical Archaeology*, Vol. 32:1, pp. 91–110 (2003)

Menuge, Adam, 'Patriotic Pleasures: Boathouses and Boating in the English Lakes' in Brandwood, Goff (ed.) *Living, Leisure and Law Eight Building Types in England 1800–1914* (Reading: Spire Books Ltd, 2010)

Ricauti, Thomas James, *Sketches for Rustic Work; including bridges, park and garden buildings, seats and furniture. With descriptions and estimates of the buildings* (London: H. G. Bohn, 1842)

Rodger, Nicholas Andrew Martin, *The Safeguard of the Sea. A Naval History of Britain*, Vol. 1, 1660–1649 (London: HarperCollins, 1997)

Rowntree, Diana, 'Oxford College Barges Their History and Decay, and Their Successors the Boathouses' in *The Architectural Review (London)*, 1956–07, Vol. 120 (714), pp. 37–42

Sherrif, Clare, *Boathouses* (London: Unicorn Press, 2008)